WOT A WAY TO RUN A WAR!

Wot a Way to Run a War!

The World War II Exploits and Escapades of a Pilot in the 352nd Fighter Group

BY TED FAHRENWALD

AUTHOR OF
*Bailout Over Normandy: A Flyboy's Adventures
with the French Resistance and
Other Escapades in Occupied France*

CASEMATE
Philadelphia & Oxford

Published in the United States of America and Great Britain in 2014 by
CASEMATE PUBLISHERS
908 Darby Road, Havertown, PA 19083
and
10 Hythe Bridge Street, Oxford, OX1 2EW

Copyright 2014 © Madeleine Fahrenwald

ISBN 978-1-61200-254-5
Digital Edition: ISBN 978-1-61200-192-0

Cataloging-in-publication data is available from the Library of Congress and
the British Library.

10 9 8 7 6 5 4 3 2 1

Printed and bound in the United States of America.

For a complete list of Casemate titles please contact:

CASEMATE PUBLISHERS (US)
Telephone (610) 853-9131, Fax (610) 853-9146
E-mail: casemate@casematepublishing.com

CASEMATE PUBLISHERS (UK)
Telephone (01865) 241249, Fax (01865) 794449
E-mail: casemate-uk@casematepublishing.co.uk

Contents

Graduation 1942: Ted gets his wings at Thunderbird Field, and his younger sister Caroline is there for the occasion. While the letters were written with the whole family in mind, many of them were addressed to "Toots."

Introduction

Composed on a borrowed Olympia typewriter in a hard-to-heat, smoke-filled Nissen hut at Bodney Airfield, England, circa 1944— amidst a riot of poker games, uninhibited quaffing, and occasional gunplay—each of this flyboy's letter-essays are literary gems that reveal in hilarious detail the daily escapades of a typical squadron of young, brash, wickedly smart American hot-shot fighter pilots. This book offers a delightful opportunity to join in the exploits of this natural-born comic writer and his squadron as they complete their flight training and make the transition to the ETO. Bicycle rides into the countryside (with plenty of stops at the pubs), clandestine small-game hunting, nightly parties in the Officers' Club, chaotic trips to Norwich and London, and of course the serious business of flying bomber escorts and strafing missions over the Continent . . . The author's meticulous, often politically incorrect, and always incisive descriptions were intended to show the folks back home the zone where booze, babes, cigarettes, insubordination, and general irreverence clashed with an American front focused on promoting patriotic values and war bonds. The cry "Wot a way to run a war!" was increasingly heard among servicemen around the world as they confronted the demons of war: Nazis, Baatan, bureaucracy, and for pilots in particular, naughty cockpit gremlins.

Ted's sheer exuberance spills over into his lyrical, in-depth narratives on flying both the Thunderbolt and Mustang, bringing to life the love of flight and the exciting rigors of air combat. The author also provides entertaining snapshot descriptions of many of his squadron-mates and leaders, each profile offering insight into the grit and audacity of the men who later became known as the Greatest Generation.

Raised in an extended Great Plains family stretching from Chicago to Idaho, Ted grew up hunting, fishing, camping, and traveling the dirt roads across 1920s and '30s America. He acquired both a private and commercial pilot's license while ostensibly attending Carleton College; for this adventuresome young man, dropping out of his journalism program and enlisting in the Army Air Corps was a no-brainer, and he brought his flying, writing, and refined prankster skills along with him. After the war, Ted returned home to run the family's specialty steel business with his brother. But in the meantime, the air over Europe was his playground.

The letters end dramatically on D-Day+2 when Ted's beloved P-51, The Joker, was mortally wounded as the truck he was strafing blew up under him. The plane crashed next to a German airdrome in Occupied Normandy while Ted parachuted to terra firma nearby. The ensuing adventure is related in his book "Bailout Over Normandy: A Flyboy's Adventures with the French Resistance and Other Escapades in Occupied France."

After reading these essays, the reader will be primed to hike side-by-side with Ted through the French countryside as he dodges Jerry encampments, assumes an adjunct career as a saboteur, carouses with Resistance fighters, escapes the deadly snare of a Wehrmacht POW camp, and treks through the French backwoods to rejoin his squadron, part of the famed 352nd.

This pilot's *joie de vivre* shines off the page, and it's impossible to read these essay-letters without grinning—and taking enormous pride in another heretofore untold story of the Allied victory in Europe.

Chapter 1

....

Training in the U.S.A.

Lt. TPF
486 Fighter Sqdn.
Republic Field
Farmingdale, Long Island

April 2, '43

E ver hear of the mischievous rascals from the land of the Leprechauns and Pixies? Well, hi-diddle-dee-dee, I have. These small characters are the gremlins who plague fighter pilots with their corny little stunts. Now just the other night, while flying at 6,000 feet over Long Island, I jumps up in my cockpit and by straining my eyes I can make out a very fantastic sight. For there perched upon the cowling and braced against the wind is one of these fabulous critters with a paintbrush in one hand and a bucket of oil in the other. This little jerk proceeds to paint my windshield black, and when finished with this thorough task he dumps what oil he has left all over the fuselage and creeps down through the air-scoop and into the engine of my now blacked-out Thunderbolt.

Down there he evidently calls in the reserves, for one small gremlin couldn't possibly make such a racket. Anyway, they gang up and poke holes in my oil lines, pump quantities of nauseous smoke into the cockpit, spit hot oil spray into my eyes, and then tear a cylinder head off my engine. Whereupon ol' Ted in the cockpit howls imprecations, fills the air with curses, and radios down to Mitchell Tower to turn on the cockeyed flood-lights and prepare for an emergency landing.

At this point, a good gremlin appears from a vacant hole in my instrument panel and perches upon my head. He lays there on his little stomach, curled around my helmet, and whispers into my earphones, telling me just when to turn and dump my gear and cut my speed, and just when to cut my switches. So with one eye hanging out in the breeze, I howl in, dust off some hi-tension lines, and set 'er down three points on the runway (tail-wheel, wingtip, one main-wheel) and call it quits. So I dead-stick in at Mitchell one dark night, and safely—thanks to my little pal.

Gremlins certainly are versatile. Some whisper at pilots. Other beat great holes in airplanes. Still others roll up the runways when a pilot tries to land, thus forcing him to give 'er the gun and go around again. This last stunt is quite novel, I think, particularly when one is equipped with a hot airplane and a cold engine. Sometimes two gremlins will perch, one on either shoulder of a pilot, when he's trying to land under difficulties. One, at the crucial moment, will holler, "Pull it up, fool!" and the other at the same time will snarl, "Set 'er on the ground, gutless!" So you see what we have to contend with. The ones I like best are those gremlins who swing from the latch of the sliding canopy when flying weather is good and everything runs smoothly. They swing to and fro singing, "Hi-diddle-dee, it's the pilot's life fer me!"

I could go on for a day about gremlins of different tribes and customs, but enuf for now. (I have seen some of 'em who swing from the snouts of the wing machine-gun and stick their little thumbs into the muzzles— which causes the guns to jam.)

By the way, on a flight a few days ago four of us get into a rat-race over NYC and dip down low and do a bunch of steep turns around the Empire State building about on a level with the 80th floor. I can see people scampering around poking their little white faces outta the windows and waving at us like folks gone mad. Hoho! Good-looking blonde stenog. working the west side near the top. Also toured thru Central Park, which is a box-canyon affair, open on one end and closed on three by tall banks of buildings. We take our four ships down in trail into the open end and pull straight up the blind wall at the far end. So then we cruise over and drop down alongside Lady Liberty, just to look over the situation. From there we see a Clipper plane, so naturally we bounce it without mercy. Swoop down on his tail and peel away so close I can count the stars on the flag painted on the side. (This treatment aggravates pilots of bombers and other trolley cars, because they envy fighter pilots like mad. We are naturally 100% more skillful flyers. We gotta be, because we fly straight up and down and upside down and whoop around like drunken eagles, while they just sit and sit and fly straight and level, hour after hour, with about fifty tons of sluggish aircraft strapped to the back of their lap.) Gee, we have fun. Everybody in this outfit loves to fly, and would rather be seen on the ground than caught in a transport type. Ha.

Our squadron CO, Bill Hennon, disappeared the other day. Took off on a routine cross-the-Sound flight and ain't been heard from since. Right after he got off, one of these infamous Long Island pea-soup fogs socked in tight. A great guy he was, with 22 Jap planes to his credit. One of the 10 top fighter aces in the Air Corps.

Should have been in combat six months ago, but things move slowly in a P-47 squadron. New ship and full of bugs (which we've been discovering the hard way). We've been flying in stuff that has the seagulls walking. Methinks they'd better ship us out quick, while there's some of us left to play.

April 6, '43

Really been getting some flying done: good weather at last—bright and sunny with white clouds and a forty-mile wind for the past three days.

We got in some green pilots—guess they brought in a dozen or so as replacements. We're a little irritated, for we were primed for combat and now another delay while these jerks build up their flying time to match ours. Also they've been busting up our pet flying machines. Matter of fact, I busted up a '47 this morning.

We flew an alert mission out over West Point and I led the second element of four ships. The guy flying my wing was one of these new jockeys. So when we land I am number three, and set down on the old runway neatly. Then I take a look into my rear-vision mirror and wot do I see but a large radial engine and twelve-foot prop that is increasing in size very rapidly. A P-47 bearing down upon me from the rear. Here's this guy and he's landed much too close behind me and too fast. So I give my ship full throttle and kick her off the runway and he scoots past my tail with an inch to spare. So there am I doing 80 or 90 mph across field and stream, and I see a revetment looming up in front of me. I put on brakes and nose over, and in this awkward position I slide into said revetment. Bust up a propeller and various odds and ends. Hi ho. Another fifth-second on the runway and my ship would have been sliced in thin slices, which would have been decidedly unpleasant.

This is the fourth Thunderbolt I've busted up, and this is the second time it ain't been my own fault. The Colonel congratulates me, this time, for quick thinking, and the other guy has been discarded from the squadron. So you see life around here is full of fun, with never a dull moment . . .

April 13, '43

A warm Spring day with the sun a-shinin' and the sky full of white clouds and airplanes, and a forty-mile wind for the past three days. Also our squadron got in twelve brand-new P-47s, right off the assembly line, and we gotta run tests on 'em and then I'll be getting one of 'em for my own, which isn't hard to take.

Republic Aircraft factory is here on our field and Grumman Aircraft is some five miles to the west, so there's a lot of rivalry between us. We jump their ships and they bust up our formations. The other day my flight was cruising along under the overcast at 3,000 feet and we spot six Wildcat fighters below us, so nacherly we peel off in line-astern, making for them. We mix it up royally for a while and then six more '47s join in, making 16 fighters whirling around and around chasing each other inside of a half-cubic-mile of fresh air. Like a bunch of drunken goldfish looping and spiraling around inside their bowl of water. Never saw so much action in so short a time. Funny part of these fights is that they bust up as quickly as they form. One second the sky is full of ships, and the next you're straining your eyes trying to find one ship to tack onto.

This morning flew an alert flight looking for an unidentified submarine, but never found it, so proceeded to fight amongst ourselves. Chased tails a while, then peeled off and down in a tremendous power dive from 17,000 clear down to the ground, and at the bottom when I peeled out my airspeed read somewhere above 500. These new ships have an airspeed indicator that registers up to 700 mph. Wheeeee.

A few minutes ago was up in a two-place AT-6 with a feller for a little instrument practice . . . but instead we checked each other out on various reckless acrobatics. Also caught a torpedo boat out on the Sound and gave him a good buzzing.

April 22, '43

Colby, Heller, Ray Barnes and me go up to 33,000 feet and fool around for a while. Colby peels off pretty steep, then Heller follows a bit steeper, then I rack 'er down a bit steeper to close up, then Barnes points 'er straight down to catch up. My controls freeze solid and I'm on the fringes of a phenomenon known as compressibility, so I forget about all else and try to save my hide. Full throttle, and I put both feet on the instrument panel and pull back on the stick as hard as I can. Controls are solid as though set in concrete, except for sudden violent tail flutters that batter the rudders back and forth. But then the nose begins to come up a fraction and I regain control and I am very happy, for few pilots have come out of such a dive, conditions governing which are quite unknown as yet. I return to the field and set down, and before long the telephone rings and some character wants to report a meteor hitting the ground. Well, Colby and Heller and me are on the ground, and that leaves Barnes, so we take off again and look for his ship and find a deep crater in the ground.

Since he and I bunked together and were close friends, I'll escort him home to his folks up near Vancouver. That makes number eight for the squadron. Five others have quit, which leaves 11 out of the original 24 pilots.

May 7, '43

Swell to be back in the swing of things again. Two weeks on the dirty old ground is a long, long time. Flew five hours yesterday and five today and my hand is back in and hot. We have all new ships now, and there's plenty of stuff in 'em. A flock of West Pointers are on the field taking their advanced flight training and the traffic pattern is a mess . . . trainers and fighters galore.

Not much news. As usual, things are never dull around here. Last night was sitting in my room in our shantytown barracks playing cards with Joe Gerst. When the lights flickered out I hollers to Joe . . . Hey Joe, some jerk just flew thru the power lines! And what do you know? Some jerk did. Undershot his landing due to the dark and stormy night and careened his fat '47 thru the high-tension lines bordering the edge of the field. Then bounced off the highway and thru a cyclone fence onto the runway. Beat the hell out of his ship, but didn't hurt the pilot much.

The other day Joe, after towing target for our aerial gunnery, buzzed the field and pulled the lever that is supposed to release the long cable and sleeve-target. Then he peeled up, dumped his gear, and came in to land. But the cable-release didn't work and Joe dragged the cable, plus a fifty-pound lead weight, down thru Republic's parking lot—beating in some fifty shiny auto tops, hoods, windshields, etc.—and then dragged it thru a sentry box, wherein was sitting a sentry. The lead weight snatched the sentry box away and demolished it, and the sentry they found still sitting on his stool, speechless from fear. Joe said ha ha ha ha! Best joke he ever saw!

May 15, '43

Been plenty busy lately, but not too busy to keep out of mischief. Fly some four missions daily, each of about an hour and a half. Past week or so have been doing a lot of legalized hedge-hopping, which we call simulated ground strafing. Go up to about 20 feet and strike out across forest and stream looking for targets. Trains and truck convoys, farmhouses and swank L.I. country-club hotels, etc. Buzz many small fishing boats and freighters, warships, subs, etc. This kind of stuff takes a very steady hand, for when clipping the treetops at 300 mph, things go by in a helluva hurry. One must keep a sharp lookout ahead for high-lines, radio towers, etc. And also when over the beach or water one must beware of the countless seagulls, which if hit will beat great holes in wings and cowling or go thru the greenhouse. Joe Gerst hit a flock of gulls one day when we were stationed at Trumbull Field, Conn. and they wrecked his ship to the tune of about 5,000 bucks of the taxpayers' moolah.

Been drawing overseas equipment, and things are coming to a focus along that line. Probably be in this country another six weeks—which is purely speculative. I think they'll fly the pilots over and send the rest of the squadron over in a boat. Holy smokes, would I hate to slop along over miles and miles of ocean in a slow old boat. Wots more, none of us daring aeronauts would care to be awakened in the middle of the night by a torpedo. That ain't our line.

Rumors are flying these days. We have helmets and .45s and rubber dinghys for our parachutes. I think we'll wind up in England. Our bombers over there have been taking a beating, and our work here as of now has been experimental very-high-altitude stuff. That plus a lot of low-level strafing missions on fancy ground targets at the tip of Long Island. So maybe we'll escort bombers to Germany and strafe our way home. Who kin tell?

Joe Gerst was one of Ted's party pals from his early days with the 486th stateside, and also a member of C Flight. He scored an aerial victory just before D-Day.

May 22, '43

Enclosed find key to footlocker I'm shipping home. Full of excess baggage. If I'm gonna travel, I'm going light.

Saw in the papers here about that spectacular crash when the B-24 bomber flew thru that big gas-storage tank outside of Chicago airport. Must have made a dandy explosion.

Fran and I had a nice evening together in NYC. If two people ever painted a town any redder, I'd like to shake their hands.

It's rained for five days. No fly. Busy tho, collecting odds and ends they tell me I'll need overseas: helmet of tin, guns, bedroll, sleeping bag, tent, canteen, etc. Will try to get a snapshot of me duked out in all that stuff. Comical sight. I don't know why in hell they don't keep all that crap and give it to some needy gravel-kicker. All any of us in this outfit need is a P-47 wrapped around us.

May 23, '43 (Farmingdale)

Old pal McKibben and me take off in tight formation, climb to ten feet
and stay there. Off we go, whooping up and down the beaches, scaring
tourists, aircraft spotters, etc. Then we really let down, flying abreast across
Peconic Bay out towards the end of Long Island. We buzz and buzz and
I see the little strip of daylight beneath Mac's ship and the water get narrower and narrower. Hmmm, I think. He is quite low. Then there occurs
a great white wake behind Mac's ship. He has hit the water. He peels up
steeply, half out of control, and I lose him in the sun until I see a plume
of water shoot skyward like a whale's spouting

In five seconds I'm over the scene and see bubbles and oil slick. I feel
badly, and think that Mac has had it. I do a wingover and come back for
another looksee. I see the tail of one P-47 protrude from the depths. I do
another wingover and there is a yellow dinghy floating about, and Mac is
aboard waving his arms to me.

I like to've spun in (and very nearly did) for I circled and circled unable
to believe his luck. I climbed to a thousand feet and radioed New York
and they sent out an amphibian to pick him up.

That evening Joe Gerst and Mac and me and some of the boys are
out having one highball apiece, celebrating Mac's luck, and he is in fine
fettle until suddenly he begins shaking like the proverbial leaf, and then
flashes his hash. A delayed reaction to his jolting plunge.

Mac sez the crash stunned him a bit, and when he woke up there was
green water all about his canopy instead of fresh air as usual. So he un-
buckles his safety belt, and can only open his hatch half way. While squirming thru the crack he inadvertently pulls the trigger on his Mae West, which
inflates over and below the crack in the canopy. He had a bad time getting
free, but made it.

May 28, '43 (Westover Field, Mass.)

It was goodbye to Farmingdale, forever. The outfit shipped up to Westover, from whence we sprung many months ago. We flew a dozen ships
up here so as to keep our hand in while awaiting overseas orders. I drove
my '65 V-8 up, and a hilarious trip it was. Rocky and Frank Cutler and me.
After the fourth blowout we got angry (and being full of beer, too) we
beat great dents and holes in the car with crowbars, threw the hood away,
wrenched off the headlights, and I wanted to roll it down a cliff up in

Connecticut somewhere. But Cutler pleaded for the old car, and we finally got her up here. No windows, tho, and with an axe we cut a navigator's hatch in the roof. Still runs, tho.

Dog tired today. Had an experience this afternoon which leads me to believe I'm still in luck . . . involving a 450 mph corkscrew dive thru 7,000 feet of solid, thick, and turbulent cloud . . . coming out in an inverted dive 3,500 feet above the Atlantic Ocean. Wheeee . . . Brother, I was all out of control.

June 3, '43

Time in the States grows short. Will soon be lookin' down on a bunch of furriners. Can't tell you when we're leaving because I don't know . . . 24 hours or days. Since all incoming and outgoing mail, phone calls, telegrams, etc. are now censored, please no telegrams wishing me bon voyage on my summer cruise to England(?) India(?) Kiska(?) Greenland(?) Australia(?). All I can chat about is last month's weather and other similar excitin' topics. Will let you know where I am when I get there.

We're rated Combat Pilots now, and we've led a merry life since we got to Westover. Little to do, a bit of flying now and then, and every night my Ford is loaded with renegades out for a fling thru the countryside. A very efficient lot in the air, we are. Not an extra brain in the bunch.

June 4, '43

Another thriller-diller today. The three squadrons of our group flew together. Thirty-six P-47s in tight formation. At takeoff, the weather was lousy . . . very dense haze, almost a fog. Anyway, down the runway we go, one at a time and into the air. We form up in short order, and when we get upstairs the weather closes in solid. So we sit on top of the clouds at 10,000 feet, 36 of us careening around together like sheep. Then down we dive looking for the ground thru the now-heavy fog. We hit some real soup, and the squadrons (12 ships each) get separated and lost. My gang feels its way down to 1,000 feet and we kin barely see the ground and nothing out to the sides—hardly one another. We got no idea where we are, so we dip down and buzz a town looking for landmarks. No find, so off we go on instruments. Finally we spot an American Airliner and tell him we're lost and low on gas, and to lead us somewhere, hey?

So we let our wheels and flaps down in order to slow down to his low speed and he leads to Hartford, and from there we follow the Conn. River up to Westover and land. All of us wringing wet from honest sweat and very low on fuel. Ho ho ho . . .

Ted's best pal and flight-mate Don "Mac" McKibben and his crew. L to R: Richard Linn, Armorer; Luman Morey, Crew Chief; Mac; and "Swen" Swenkowski, Assistant Crew Chief.

June 9, '43

This is nice country in the summer—fine to fly over, and am surprised at the great forested area up here. Flying up along the Conn. River I've seen some fine country. There are rolling hills and a small range of mountains north of here; up towards New Hampshire and Vermont is beautiful land. Lots of small blue lakes and rivers with white rapids in them where they flow thru the passes in the hills. Really didn't know this country until I'd flown across it. Can't judge it by the big towns. Springfield is just another dirty city (even if one of my ancestors did found the place!) But buzzing low on cross-country flights I see some of the quaintest damn villages— each with a narrow main street and white church with small graveyard alongside.

Getting some choice weather now . . . sunny days and a blue sky full of white clouds to play around in. Got Spring fever as usual, and for once can do something about it. Used to sit and gaze at those clouds and wish I could careen around the lumps and humps on 'em. Now I can climb into my '47 and in nuthin' flat I'm up right in amongst 'em! Great fun to scoot down the white canyons and plunge into a big fat bulge on a cloud. Like to see the shadows of clouds moving across the green hills below.

Things in a turmoil around here. Squadron is packed and set to light out on an hour's notice.

June 16, '43

When you get this letter, I'll be elsewhere. Outfit is moving to Port of Embarkation, so this will be the last letter for two or three weeks, and find myself forced to smuggle this one out.

An easy life now. Nice weather and nothing to do but loaf. We got rid of the V-8—or rather the gendarmes got it. We filled it with bullet holes from our .45s and drenched it with chicken blood and left it on the highway to give the local flatfeet something to ponder.

Next time I fly it'll be over strange country. Have a fair idea of where we're going. Tally Ho!

The gang spent last night in the Club here, drinking beer and whisky and having a gay old time. Back in our BOQ, about midnight, the party degenerated into a pitched battle involving fire extinguishers, buckets, thousands of gallons of branch water, etc. Very amusing. At one a.m. the flight surgeon was forced to journey to the hospital for a supply of bandages and iodine. But today we shelled out $202.30 to pay for new walls, etc. And our boy Cutler shelled out $75 for shooting all the knotholes out of the floor with his .45. Wheee. We are eager to get the hell out of here and quit wasting our time.

We ran barber's shears thru one anothers' fur, too. Much fun for the audience and some rare effects, indeed. Look like an outlaw gang for sure, now. Gave my gittar to a Spaniard mechanic named Ramirez (no kidding). He kin wallop the daylights out of one, and he sings, too.

Rocky and I have taken four mechanics for rides in our two-seater AT-6 and gotten three of 'em sick. Pretty good percentage. Rather a mean trick, but kinda fun, too. The last one bet a dollar on the deal and he did last for a half hour of wicked stunts. But I looks in the mirror at him and he looks very pale and peaked, and finally I whip thru three fast and sloppy barrel rolls and sure enuf, he outs with his cookies. Ho ho ho!

Had some thunderstorms lately, and sounds good to hear the old rumbling again. Have flown thru some storms but have never seen this St. Elmo's fire they say will sometimes dance on the prop and wings.

We've had to strip our uniforms of all insignia. No wings, no Air Corps shoulder patches, no Air Corps rings, etc. and the uniform of the day is strictly soldier: tin hat, backpack, pistol, canteen, etc. Khaki stuff with laced leggins' and GI clodhoppers. For, you see, nobody is supposed to know we are a fighter outfit . . . supposed to think we're infantry or something. But if you see a gang of exceedingly sloppy soldiers making big talk and diving and zooming with their hands and craning their necks at the first sound of a faraway plane, then you'll know they're not soldiers, but throttle-jockeys traveling incognito.

Ted sporting the "crusher" look.

Chapter 2

∙ ∙

"Over Strange Country"

July 9th—England

Quite a gap in our correspondence, but it seems that there has occurred a slight geographical gap consisting of a considerable stretch of salt water called the Atlantic Ocean. Had an uproarious good time getting here, seeing much that is pleasant to look back upon—numerous natural-sevens, a full-house or two, a whale, a porpoise, a seasick Colonel, and more of which I'll be able to relate only after the war. So now have seen some intriguing country through which I hanker to prowl someday at my leisure. And I would like to poke through some of the impressive, story-book castles—all gloomy and foreboding and perched atop the highest cliffs.

We're stationed at an old and luxurious RAF airdrome—the best quarters our tired squadron has seen to date, and we're close enough to London that an occasional venture into town will be possible. Norwich and Cambridge are less far away and will no doubt be the scene of many an interesting and educational evening. Have chatted with pilots of England, Canada, New Zealand, and Australia and Africa, and no doubt I'll run across a few old flying pals from Chicago.

All in this country is on strict wartime basis, with every yard and bit of land a garden, rationing no joke, and all the gals in uniform. For they conscript all tamales in this neck of the woods.

Have had a reckless time with my money here trying to figure out pounds, shillings, and pence, and I've come now to the point where when I buy a glass of suds I just hold out a handful of chicken-feed and let the innkeeper take what he pleases. Wonder what I've been paying for beer of late?

Oddly, it doesn't get dark until after midnight and by six a.m. it's broad daylight again. A long summer day, and in wintertime, I presume, a correspondingly long night.

July 18, '43

My theory that the Army sometimes operates in reverse is now borne out. Having taken its heavy losses back in the States, the squadron has been sent to "combat" in England for a rest cure. We find ourselves a fighter outfit without sufficient aircraft, and so there have been no major casualties of late—something of a novelty. But we have each been issued a fine bicycle, and with them we have been terrorizing the natives throughout a ten-mile radius.

We're busy from six to six—flying a bit and soaking up advice and intelligence from local hot-shots—and then for the long evening, we're free to explore. So out we head through the countryside, a few of us pedaling in fancy formation, and since this bicycle business involves the expenditure of considerable physical effort and perspiration, you may assume that each pub encountered en route is hit for a mug or two or three of strong ale. And while our outbound course is always navigated with skill and ease, the return trip is unfailingly hilarious—especially after nightfall.

Now, these country inns are happy social institutions of a thousand year's standing, and they run to fancy names: Red Lion, Bristly Boar, Golden Swan, Pig's Eye, Hefty Heifer, Blue Goose, etc. Of an evening the local old folks trudge down the roads and drift in to shoot darts and hash over the day's proceedings while slopping up the vile brew. I find it rather amusing to watch a bunch of eighty-year-old ladies sitting around a sticky table telling their corny jokes, talking war news, and cackling into their pints of half-and-half.

Now and then I stop along the road to neighbor with a farmer, and so have met some rare birds. They tell me how they armed themselves with iron fence-pickets and patrolled the country lanes when invasion was threatened during the Battle of Britain. The fields of small grain and truck-garden stuff are just about ready for harvesting, and it's a shame to see the damage done by the thousands of maneuvering tanks.

Aerial navigation here is a bit difficult due to the endless hodge-podge of crooked roads and oddly shaped fields. In the States, you know, all the country is surveyed and laid out in sections with roads running north and south, east and west. But here from the air one sees thousands of tiny fields running endlessly together, and the general effect is one large jigsaw puzzle. There are few landmarks, and one must remember the shape of the various local forests, and the boys are all the time getting lost. I had to stop in at a strange airdrome this morning and inquire the way home.

We're doing our flying from a small grass field, which is easier to fly from and more fun than flying off narrow concrete runways. Here you just shove throttle and let'er flicker. Take-off is over the crest of a sizeable hill, and the crest is met when the take-off run is about half complete. The effect is that of a catapult, and an addition has been made to the already terrific sport of flying these Thunderbolts.

Last night being Saturday night, Willie O. Jackson and McKibben and I put on our glad rags and took out for Norwich. And a quaint city it is, old as the hills and full of sights for us tourists. Got trapped in an ancient castle, and later an old dame who ran a pub told me that it was built seven or eight hundred years ago by a few generations of slaves. Quite a chore to haul such mighty stone blocks up without any fancy machinery. Old serfs must have led a tough life.

Had an excellent chicken dinner, complete with feathers and silverware (for two shillings extra) and served by a charming lassie who I later escorted to a local shindig. Clumped merrily around the floor for a few hours and had a dandy time. Wish to hell it'd get to be winter, however. Damn sun didn't go down until after I took this queen to her flat. Helluva thing.

July 22, '43
Right at this moment am sitting in a hut in the middle of a green and cool forest, and outside the sun shines brightly in patches between the trees. The boids is choipin' in the brush and wee rabbits scuttle aimlessly about. At any moment I fully expect Robin Hood and his Merrie Men to taxi through the area—which would be quite a deal, allright.

Am soon to move into a Nissen hut with some of the gang. Now these huts are nothing but an overgrown section of sewer pipe with the ends boarded up to keep folks from wandering through on their way to town. We look forward to moving into them, though, as we are getting fed up with leading the life of luxury which is ours over at this old RAF base.

Over there we must dress for dinner and suck on a teacup twice per day. Over there, too, we pilots each have what they call a "Batman." Now don't be misled by this quaint name, as I was. From my extensive reading of Komic Kartoon Books back in the States, I was under the impression that a Batman was the character who would whisk his cloak around his shoulders and with a perfectly hideous shriek perform some fantastic job of flying without an airplane under him. But in this land of mystery, the batman performs such menial tasks as making beds and serving tea and pressing my britches. Hi ho.

Just had a flight in a large U.S. transport plane—the purpose being to familiarize us with the surrounding terrain without becoming lost in the process. Saw much of interest: old castles and fancy chateaux and towns protected by fat and silvery barrage balloons.

(I find this to be a very irritating typewriter due to the fact that the blamed thing sticks, and especially the letter "A", which is looking for trouble in a big way . . .)

Only damages sustained by yers truly to date in this vicious battle for aerial supremacy are (1) cut finger incurred while opening can of GI rations at midnight while using hunting knife for can-opener and (2) bashed fingernail incurred during squadron beer party when Parchesi-Joe Gerst slammed window on finger (mine.)

July 25, '43

Hope that Tommy Price's P-47 outfit doesn't go through the endless months of shuffling around that ours has before he gets into combat. Afraid he has much to learn of the slow-grinding mill of the AAF. We're getting a few new ships in now and shouldn't have much longer to wait.

Things going slowly, but have flown enough to keep my hand in. Just enough action to keep things from becoming monotonous. Flew an hour or so today and never did get over ten feet altitude. Ol' Joe Gerst gave us a buzz job this afternoon, the likes of which nobody ever could see again. He brought that old Thunderbolt around through a couple of hangars, under an apple tree, and between two chimneys on the roof of this RAF officer's club. The chimneys are just about forty feet apart, and Joe's wingtips took the dust off the bricks on either side. We're all hotter'n two-dollar pistols, and if we don't get into combat pretty soon we'll just have to start fightin' amongst ourselves.

Chapter 3

. . . .

At Bodney Airfield

July 29, '43

Weather superb, probably because we have insufficient aircraft in which to fly combat. Warm and sunny most every day and I'm feelin' so ornery I kin hardly stand it.

Have moved from the RAF base at Watton to our own little AAF field, which is tucked into the edge of a great woods. Our luxury quarters have turned into a shantytown deal, and the wild bunch now lives together in a corrugated iron pipe. But we like it much better, having now gotten away from the dress-for-dinner, tea-at-11-and-4 stuff. Seven of us living in this hut, and all survivors of the old Fightin' 21st outfit of our shabby seashore fighter-strip at Groton, Ct. And all of us lieutenants, with time-eroded, salt-corroded bars on shoulders: Parchesi-Joe Gerst, Big Ed Heller, Lloyd Archibal Rauk (!), Bottle-Arse Leo Northrop, Brown, and old pal Mc-Kibben. Wot a bunch. Cook up something different every night.

Like last night, the bunch of us goes rabbit hunting out in a local turnip patch with blood in our eyes and .45 pistols in hand. Armed to the teeth we are, and we fill the air with whoops and howls and singing lead. But get nary a rabbit. Tonight Rocky and me cycle about 15 miles, looking over the lay of the land. We have a few gallons of strong ale and mild beer at wayside inns and pedal through a river and come back to the hut at midnight to find a red-hot poker game in session. Being broke, however, I write this letter instead of joining in, and am writing on the back of my gittar in the absence of other furniture.

Got well lost flying the other day in the haze, but after much churning around and many confused glances at my charts I got home intact. Would hate to get lost and set down on some Jerry airdrome in France. It's just a few minutes flight across the narrow neck of the English Channel, and it's been done by both RAF and Jerry fighter pilots. Most humiliatin'.

Right now somebody has a Jerry propaganda program on the radio, and it is quite good: tall tales, atrocious lies, and wild claims interspersed with the latest stateside music. And the night skies above our tiny hut are filled with the roar of RAF bombers beamed on the Continent. When a flock of those heavies go over, the sound is that of a second Niagara Falls, and not at all like the whistling whir of our fast fighters.

You will note in your papers at home that the AAF is pasting the day-lights out of France, Germany, and points east, and during daylight hours. Also, you will note that the old Thunderbolt (with which one Fighter Group over here is equipped) is showing up well in combat and promises to be the best of its type in any theater.

We've been eating like kings of late. Pilots get fresh eggs three times a week for breakfast. And the saddened ground officers sit and watch us eat 'em, while they sit and chomp mournfully upon their dehydrated, syn-thetic-rubber-type eggs. Ho ho ho.

Seeing as how there was gonna be a war, I sure got into the right racket. Very few characters these days are now doing what they have always wanted to do most of all.

Am busy every day, all day, and have enjoyed my spare time to the ut-most. It's good to be away from cities and back in the open air. The Back to Nature movement is in full swing . . .

Aug. 4, '43

One day has been running into the next with astounding ease. The nights are getting chilly again and before long, winter. Phooey. You folks have it easy as compared to these English people. They can't get much of anything anymore, and terrific prices are paid for the little luxuries. Everybody and his Uncle rides a bicycle here, too: old jerks with their beards streaming back in the wind. . . . fat old women whose fannies flop down a foot on either side. . . . little children on wee machines pedal madly along the roads, but the best of all is to see some gal wheeling to market with her baby rid-ing a basket atop the rear fender. Some streamlined papoose!

Big poker game last night. Had a flight party in our hut and we mixed up a batch of panther . . . er, joy-juice, that is, and played cards till dawn. Play a lot of cards around here: casino, poker, blackjack, red-dog, etc., shoot darts, play checkers and cribbage, plus a lot of night-riding on two wheels.

Our fighter group, you know, is of three squadrons. Two squadrons' pilots and half of our own live in a fine old chateau nearby, which used to belong to some millionaire Duke or something of the sort. Clermont Hall, they call it, and quite a layout it is. A beautiful place with miles and miles of grounds around it, including forests of giant elms and large grain fields . . . a shooting preserve and the whole works, complete with a multitude of fat cock-pheasants (upon which I have my eye.) But in our little hut at the edge of the field here, our little crew of exiles can live as sloppy as we danged well please, which is quite. A couple of characters come in now and then to sweep and so on, but we manage to keep a few jumps ahead of their aimless efforts. We pay 'em off in our brand of cigarettes, which beats their own by a mile.

They've got this flying down to a science over here. Every precaution for the pilot's sake is taken and there is a special bus daily to pick pore pilots out of the North Sea and English Channel. The other day, after a big daylight raid, this Air-Sea Rescue outfit fished some 250 U.S. airmen outta the North Sea.

On that same raid, a group of Thunderbolts of the 8th Fighter Command knocked down twenty-five of Herman Goering's best FW-190s.

Still am trying to find a suitable name for my ship. A fitting one eludes me. All the ones I think of are profane.

Aug. 12, '43

When I last wrote I don't recall, but here's another fer ye anyway. Just back from 48 hours well spent in London town. And I do mean spent. Pound notes go like bucks in NYC, and my soft stuff was unloaded in short order. Puttered around Picadilly and got a little looped on ale, then went and poked around the old shops and had my watch strap patched by an old bird who makes saddles and belts in a cellar joint that's been on location for at least five hundred years. Got a big kick out of the taxicabs in that town—all alike and all look to be fifty years old and are utterly devoid of any semblance of streamlines. All are piloted by ancient, skinny, white-

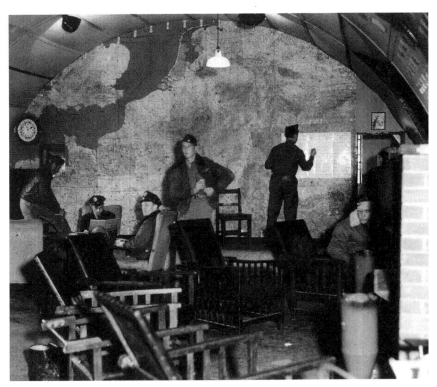

The 486th Squadron's Ready Room and Lounge.

haired old gnomes who wear caps and who also look exactly alike. They sit there behind their wheels and stare straight ahead thru their glasses, looking neither left nor right, but boring thru traffic disregarding all about them. An independent lot they are, too. The meters, however, are quite like our own, even if they do tick away counting off pennies and shillings rather than cents and dollars. Wot a system.

Hotels are filled all the time, but the day is saved by the Red Cross clubs, which offer a bed for three shillings and good chow for two. All served (meals) by lovely English lassies who smile sweetly and roll their eyeballs at the lads. Somewhere along the line of our travels, a couple of the boys and I pass in front of a palace or something. In front of which are a few very hefty soldiers dressed up in an outlandish rig: big plumed hats, etc. These jerks are standing guard at a rigid position of parade-rest with their rifles thrust out in front of them. When we come by, these guards burst into violent activity, stamping their boots and making little hops up into the blue and throwing their rifles around in a reckless manner. This energizing finally results in a verra fancy salute—which we acknowledge, somewhat bewilderedly, with a raunchy and nonchalant Air Corps-type salute. So we proceed around town, noting the gaps in blocks caused by bombs. The rubble is cleared away after each raid, and all that remains of the many demolished buildings is busted-up cellar walls and scarred-up surrounding walls.

We meet up with some jerk of an American chairborne trooper, an officer from some London HQ who proceeds to chat airily with us using a recently acquired British accent. So we drop our H's recklessly and discuss the price of tea and the Indian situation with wild abandon, until this gent catches on to the razz and stutters that it really was quite 'ard not to pick up a bit of the of accent, y'know. I figger our talk to be good enuf, ain't it so?

Up in Norwich the other day the Yank soldiers put on a rodeo show complete with bucking horses ridden by the best talent from our Southwest. The Englishmen went nuts when they saw it. Most amazing thing they'd ever seen. My word. Such goings on, and on a cricket field, too.

Inactivity is ours of late. Going slightly nuts from the lack of flying. So if I don't fall into a cellar pub some black night and bust me neck, you may rest assured that no harm shall come to this dejected character. There'll come the day, no doubt, but I sure hate laying around. Spend all my time thinking up mischief. Having been the chief backer for a powerful crap game some weeks ago, I ain't got the capital necessary to operate as operating should be done. I would holler for a natural and snake eyes would stare at me. Then changing tactics, I would holler for snake eyes. And guess what would turn up? Yer right. Snake eyes. And the London journey took the rest of my slim roll down the line.

I sit here, running short on talk, in me little sewer pipe with me hat on backwards. Joint is littered with flying clothes and cigarette butts and empty bottles, etc. By the way, you would enjoy this place, I know. The other morning I lifted my weary carcass out of my cot and there, cuddled up under to keep warm, were two red beetles (with little pincers on their behinds) and one rather large black caterpillar. Ha!

And all the little urchins around here stop me on the streets to holler in their teeny piping voices, "Hey Yanks! Gottny chewn gum, hey?" or they holler, "Hey Yank! Gimme American money, hey?" I mutter "Run along, bud, run along," and they retreat to a respectful distance and hurl vile threats at me.

Also the local tea shops are manned (or womanned) by elderly Janes, mostly, and they are stunned to see us surreptitiously snake out a bottle of whiskey and pep the tea up a little. Really does, you know?

They got our ships scientifically camouflaged, and on top of that they have painted tremendous and colorful white stars of the AAF. White stars bordered by a wide red band. Also wide white bands are painted around the fuselage and nose to aid in instant, distant identification

Bought a first-class ticket to London, and the damn train was so full of folks I rode the way on top of a milk-can in the baggage car. But it still doesn't spoil my philosophy: "Wot the hell. It doesn't cost much more to go first class."

Aug. 15, '43
Nothing much from this neck of the woods to report. Got a good chance to look over a flock of Allied and Jerry fighters . . . Spits, Typhoons, Hurricanes, Mustangs, Me-109s, and FW-190s, etc. All to aid in instant identification. Fighters look quite a bit alike when viewed momentarily at closing speeds of maybe 800 mph, and cases of mistaken identity are not uncommon and usually fatal. Also checked out in Jerry planes' cockpits, so as I kin swipe one and taxi it home should I ever find meself making an escape from Germany.

Germany seems to be taking a nice pounding from our bombers.

Any time, day or night, one can hear the Forts and RAF four-engine stuff droning eastward overhead. Sometimes in the space of a very few minutes can count 150 or 200 ships heading out on course.

Surprising the way we can identify a plane by the sound it makes going over. The bunch of us will be laying around the hut when a drone filters thru. Immediately ears are tuned in and guesses made as to what type ship it is. Then we scuttle outside and take a looksee. Generally right, too. Radial engines make an entirely different sound than an inline. We can all spot the ship we fly without any trouble. Makes a fuzzy roar. A Spit makes a whistle and a whine that is unmistakable. Our Mustangs are almost silent, but like the Spit its staccato exhaust noise is topped by a shrill whistle of geared superchargers. Bombers have their own roar, but we kin get along without them trucks in this letter. Sure glad I don't fly one. Have a helluva lot more fun with our own little rockets.

The hut is about empty tonight. Few of the lads in London looking things over. Mac and I are holding the fort. He's lying on his bunk reading "Lone Star Terror," which is a wild and woolly western pulp mag (printed in London!) Just lit up a fancy cigarette called "Abdullah's" (10 Grand Prix, four Diplomas of Honour, 23 Gold Medals.) Tastes like ragweed.

Say, here's something to write home about. A couple of nights ago, Joe Gerst and Rocky and me are merrily buzzing thru a local town on our cycles. All is dark and we are loaded and we get pinched by the local gendarme for driving without lights! My word, it's dangerous, sez the bobby. Like to take him up for a short hop in my ship some day. Ho ho ho.

Country hereabouts is full of old Roman ruins, etc. A few old windmills which I've climbed up into . . . full of ancient wooden machinery. Big wooden gears, etc.

Aug. 16, Merrie Olde

I repeat . . . you need but one air-mail stamp on yer letters to me over here, so cease your confounded extravagance, willya?

I get a terrific laff out of some of the newspaper articles in the London papers. They haggle over the most trivial items, and of late have been having a helluva time with their war, as note my quote from the enclosed clipping: it concerns the trial of some poor jerk for the crime of luring three RAF homing pigeons into his loft. The fellow seems to have a mania for pigeons. I quote: " . . . the defendant . . . said he had bought the pigeons. Witness told him he suspected him of having had two RAF pigeons in his loft recently, and Newell said that they were now in another pigeon loft in Beeching Road. He added that his cat had killed a third. He has been warned on previous occasions about his conduct with pigeons and has practically defied us. He is not considered a desirable person to keep pigeons . . . Mr. Dain (the Chief Constable) added that Newell had been sent to prison recently for assaulting his mother . . . Had a conviction for using bad language and had previously been sent to an approved school for being beyond control."

This Newell chap must be one tough hombre, allright.

Also noted a wedding announcement, which I clipped out but lost. Read something like this: "Lady and Lord Thimblebottom of Nimblewitte

Manor announce the Wedding of their Daughter Pamela, at Mumblede-peg Moors, to Sir Leonard Liverlips, Earl of Scrawnypaunch-on-the-Sea." No kidding, it ran just like that. Gimme another short tea, Mac!

Pedaled furiously over hill and dale today. Also went over to another fighter field and watched a fleet of fighters return from a haul across the Channel. Some shot up, none lost, and twenty victories.

Still pondering a name for my ship. Considered naming each gun for a gal, but there are but eight guns and I don't want to play favorites.

Time-out to build me a fire in the stove. Gettin' kind of chilly in this neck of the woods. Furthermore, if you see the initials ETO in your paper they mean European Theater of Operations, which is where I find myself.

You might send me a couple cans of Simonize. Will put it to good use waxing the wings and fuselage of my ship. Adds some 10 or 15 mph to top speed, which might be handy one time.

Party boys: Ted ("T.P.F"), Joe Gerst, and Ed Heller were flight and hut mates at Bodney Airfield; shown here with Tom Colby, a 486th squadron member.

My gittar playing has not improved one whit. However I have incorporated a fancy slide down the keyboard in my new and special corn arrangement of "San Antonio Rose." A-ronky-tonky-tonk-tonk-tonk. Ain't that awful?

Have seen no Gremlins lately. Miss the little varmints. Lt. Don Higgins of previous bailout-over-Conn. fame had another reckless flight the other day . . . flew straight thru a grove of oak trees at the end of the runway. Trees of a foot-and-a-half diameter or so. He steps out of the wreckage intact, however. Ship utterly demolished. Not a very smart thing to do. Non-habit forming.

As you kin see by the diversified subject matter herein, I am devoid of intelligent items for this evening. As I am the only gent around who can handle the French language to any extent, all the time I gotta translate little things the boys find in their intensive studies. Tonight one character asks me what "Kest lay gweer" means. I sez you mean "C'est la guerre?" And he sez yeh, I guess so. Any fool, sez I, knows it means, "Look for the woman involved."

Speaking of wimmen, all the gals here between six and sixty are drafted into the WAAFs or WRNs. (Wrens, that is.) I wonder if these English know that they talk pure Cicero (Illinois) when they speak of their Wrens? (Woman's Reserve Naval Service.) The boys back in Chi been askin' each other for years now. "Jeez youze guys . . . lamp dat wren over dere." Wren, doll, skoit, moll, frail, quail . . . sure a lotta names for you babes.

And again speakin' of wimmen, if they looked after their Wrens here as carefully as they look after their pigeons, us poor pilots would have a helluva time, come a 48-hour leave in London town . . .

Chapter 4

Chateau Life

Aug. 23, '43

Now what do you think of a place like this? Millionaire's chateau . . . forty or so rooms . . . baths with rose-colored tubs, etc., master bedroom in which any number of cats might be swung, servant's quarters, gamekeepers lodge, greenhouses, thick forest well-stocked with grouse and pheasant. Hmmmm? Well anyhow, that's where this gang is now ensconced. Moved out of our sewer pipe several days ago and into this castle where we intend to live for a long time in the manner to which we ain't accustomed. From where I sit I can look out thru three bay windows and take in a very expensive sight indeed. And expansive. Restful to the eyeballs. Below the windows, five hundred feet or so of green lawns studded with giant elms and oaks, then a solid background of deep and dark forest— mostly firs and evergreens of one kind or another. Winding graveled roads and stuff like that there. Hi ho . . . that danged gamekeeper hasn't been keeping the partridges out of the orchid garden. Guess I'll be forced to discharge him. Hi ho.

Ruff way to fight a war, is it not? Do my flying from the same field, which is reached by jeep in several minutes when there is flying to be done. Do not envy the lads who are fighting the dirty end of the war. Infantry and artillery and other ground-stricken folk like that. I live more or less the life of Reilly, just taking off from a world of quiet and restful ways and flying into the war for a brief session of dirty work, then returning to the other world. All done with a zip and a bang. The paddlefeet in the outfit even envy us our part, for they do the monotonous and necessary volumes of routine paper work and so on, while we sit back until all is planned and ready for us and then take over and trudge into battle on our 2,000 horses per each. Feel a leetle guilty now and then to ponder the life we lead, but what the hell, we sure worked to get where we are. Tallyho, we holler, and proceed to enjoy ourselves to the extreme.

You save these letters home, and when we gather round the bottle to tell our tall tales I'll use 'em to refresh my memory of some of these eventful days. Can't tell a helluva lot, either, due to the danged censors. Can't keep a diary, either.

Flew a Cub the other day. My day off, so I finagled the use of it and hopped the flight surgeon around to different fighter bases. Flew low and slow all the way and sure had a barrel of fun. Saw a most amazing sight and saw it in an amazing manner. Was in the middle of breaking the monotony by way of a few stunts, and just completed one half of a fat loop when I look up over my head at the ground to see where I am and there above me on the ground is this castle. High stone walls forming a perfect circle about a hundred yards in diameter, with some little stone buildings inside the enclosure. Turrets and the whole shooting match, and a moat around the outside edge. Had to go down and poke around for a while. This was up near the North Sea coast, not far from here. Distances in this neck of the woods are confusing. So small. At home you think of a little drive of a few hundred miles. Do that over here and you'd find yourself jumping outta the pan into the fire.

Been to London twice now and have tangled up with a very charming lassy indeed. Blonde, and her name is Lil. Short and sweet.

Perfect weather. Cool sunny days and cold nights disturbed only by the sound of bombers. Many dazzling searchlight patterns of late, and sounds of distant bombings. Many fingers of light probing thru the mists and cloud decks looking for some jerk flying around up there with a load of bombs.

Still healthy and full of la vie and lookin' for trouble. Broke right at this moment due to an unfortunate turn of the Dixie Dominoes, but payday ain't fur off . . .

Things really booming now in this outfit. The enclosed clipping reminds me of a joke where the shocked hostess at banquet asks guest why he has massaged the rootabaga into his hair. He replies in startled amazement: "Rootabaga! I thot those were cauliflower!"

Aug. 26 or 27

Several more enjoyable flights of late, and like the old '47 more all the time. A beautiful hunk of machinery. You oughta see the guts of one of 'em . . . packed solidly with guns and ammo, radio stuff and turbo accessories and engine and a thousand other Rube Goldberg devices. Most complicated little thing. Enjoy living in this shack with the gang. We have a slick deal with this chateau, and know it. Quite crowded (75 pilots) but plenty o.k. A movie every night or so down in the lounge. "Moontide" tonight, with guy named Gabin and some lovely doll. Excellent entertainment.

Food here is swell. Squadron baker used to run P.K. Wrigley's kitchen in Hawaii or some such deal. Keeps us supplied with choice pastries. Plenty wheesky and beer for them what thirst (75 pilots.) Plenty gals available for them wot craves female companionship (75 etc.) What a way to go!

One of my good friends of the squadron, Capt. Eddie Gignac, is really a character. Had quite a write-up in last month's "Esquire" as regards his sports and war record. Was a national collegiate ski-jumping champion, and is highly decorated for his feats in combat flying. He's a little guy built like a keg. Face all scarred up from various crashes, including shot down twice in New Guinea by the Nips. Anyway, Gig is a natural born clown, and is full of the wildest lying stories I've heard in a long time. Well, the other night he goes down to the kitchen. This in itself requires great skill, as Gig and me and one or two others are quite gay from having cooked up a batch of joy juice. But Gig comes back with an armful of sugar and cocoa and butter and vanilla and states that he, by god, is going to make us some fudge. So he cooks up a batch on an electric plate and soon has all our mess kits full to brimming with boiling, sticky, highly elastic fudge. Which we et in about two minutes.

You tell ol' Fran to take it a little easier on the work for a couple weeks. Got to keep him healthy. A wicked grind for him in your hot weather. He's doing more for the war effort than I, and not getting the sport out of the deal!

Got a radio now blaring out with the Nazi broadcast in English. Get a wallop out of their corny propaganda, tall tales of Luftwaffe exploits. They don't do much broadcasting from Berlin after dark, for the sounds

Ted writes that "Pappy Gignac was the squadron's pride and joy. A mischievous little rascal . . . been shot down twice in the Pacific War over New Guinea while flying P-39s against the Japs. Pappy got his face hamburgered down there, and came back to the States with a Silver Star and permanently jangles nerves. But he took over as second in command of our squadron and came to Europe with us: shot down quite a few Jerries and then was blown to smithereens when a truck he was strafing exploded under him on June 7, 1944." Ironically, the next day Ted and his plane suffered exactly the same fate, but Ted was lucky enough to have time to bail out—leading him on a three-month adventure on the ground in Occupied France and resulting in his book "Bailout Over Normandy: A Flyboy's Adventures with the French Resistance and Other Escapades in Occupied France."

of our bombs goin' off sort of spoils their denials of same.

Couple of the boys visited a B-17 base near here the other day and crawled into the nose of one ship along with the bombardier and went out sightseeing on a raid. Glad to be back on the ground, they say, but had an interesting and educational trip over the Lowlands.

Dunno why this Paul Sturger guy from Thunderbird Field wants to know so much, but if you care, write him my flying record: Thunderbird, Minter, and Luke Fields, then Trumbull, Republic, Westover Fields in P-47s, then Kilmer for POE. Now England. I'd like to run this Thunderbolt thru Thunderbird Field. When I was down there nobody ever even saw such a machine as this. Beyond me wildest dreams.

Have a dance lined up for tomorrow night, to be flung right here in our little palace. The Doc has been operating around locally lining up a bunch of gals . . . got a band coming in and little liquid cheer in the form of some medicinal alcohol from the Flight Surgeon's kit. He claims that he can blend it with various odds and ends to make a very tasty cocktail. Seems to me he mentioned oil of wintergreen, 188-proof alky, grapefruit juice, and other items. Ho ho ho. Ain't nobody gonna walk away from this 'un.

Aug. 30, '43

Hallo, Pal: not feeling like writing an intelligent letter tonight, will instead fill the page with idle thoughts . . . You probably get a gander at some of the trash I write home so by that you kin see how the Thunderbolt Branch of Fahralloy Ltd. is operating. We sure like our ship, and it never ceases to amaze me how faithfully such a complicated hunk of machinery keeps purring. In all the flying my squadron has done, here and in the States, we've had only one engine failure . . . (Guess who? Naturally it wuz me, that dark and stormy night over Mitchell Field!) I always get me mitts on something and have it disintegrate right out from under me. Remember that time I jumps into your Nash and have a wheel fall off the goddam thing? Yipe. Can recall countless other examples, which are no end amusing. Me and King Midas. Everything he touched turned to GOLD . . . everything I touch turns into JUNK. Hi ho.

This Cecil B. DeMille shack here is a bit different than that tarpaper job you spent the night in up at Trumbull Field in Conn. We have a helluva time here, you bet. Not the way we thought we'd be fighting the war. We had delightful visions of slit trenches and mad scrambles into the air between strafing attacks by enemy aircraft, etc., all done strictly blood and thunder a la Hollywood. Here we live in luxury. In class. Pleasant surroundings and so forth. Chauffeured out to the flight line early every morning. Spend a busy day flying, studying maps and tactics and gunnery, etc. and poking around the guts of my ship. Get the dirty work over in a few fast-moving hours and then cruise over to the jernt for an evening of movies, soft music, hard drinks, rattling bones, and pleasant comraderie. Wot a racket. But boy, there is sure plenty of lead flying daily over the Continent.

Forts boring to their targets, dueling continually with persistent Jerry fighters and dodging all the flak lobbed up at 'em. Thunderbolts careening up from half a dozen fields in England to do their intercepting job and fly top cover, etc. Shooting hell outta fleets of Focke-Wulfs and Messerschmidts and stuff like that. Feature a couple hundred Forts scooting along at 25,000 feet or so, with a lot of Thunderbolts flying in fours circling over 'em at 30,000 feet . . . then a bunch of Jerry fighters close in, and before they can attack our bombers a squadron of '47s detaches from the top cover and arrows in on 'em. Zonk.

By golly, hope I can swindle a couple weeks leave this winter. Ain't had a day off since before the war, I think. Shouldn't be too hard to do as days are short and nights are long in winter, and the weather is socked in most of the time. And I'll leave the night fighting up to the night-fighters. You know, it gets chilly in these parts. The latitude is about that of Labrador or the middle of Hudson Bay, or about even with the southern end of Alaska. Fifty-four degrees North, which is pretty far up.

Understand that Fahralloy is booming, thanks to your all-out, or all-in efforts. So you knocked yourself out during recent business trip to East Coast area. Well, don't push yer scrawny frame too hard, Pal. Better to have you running on both mags than to have you in the hangar for a top overhaul. Like us, we kin only push our big radials for a few minutes at top military power. Stretch 'er any more and she liable to blow ooop, leaving pilot strapped into bucket seat with throttle in one hand and stick in the other, and no airplane in sight. Also while dishing out words of wisdom, there is such a thing as pilot fatigue, whereupon a flyer gets hisself into helluva slump where nuthin' matters, and flies around like old folks making love. Loss of efficiency, etc. So then Doc has him grounded under orders to sleep, relax, and have a snort or two. But here, the only pilot fatigue (as we don't fly enuf to wear ourselves out) is caused by constant effort of sliding glasses down the bar for a refill.

If this ain't a helluva letter. Don't know any jokes, but some old Englishman I wuz chatting with the other night sez "Say, Leftenant, did you hear th' one about the embryo idjit?" No, I sez to be polite. Whereupon he wrings the suds outta his lip-spinach and sez slyly, "A little inside dope . . ." I think to meself, I thot I left all that back in the States, Migawd, and then I donate a slight chuckle, whereupon he fills the air with booming laughter, muttering, "A good 'un, a good 'un."

Sept. 2, '43

Been having a wonderful time ovah here in the old country. Weather has been tender indeed, and it is a pure joy to be alive and kicking and breathing in the sea breezes and in general admiring the wonders of Nature. Skies been blue as the waters off the coast of Florida, and the clouds have been made-to-order to explore. Spare time has been spent poking thru the local forests.

An average day, today . . . spent couple of hours lining inside rubber mat of my goggles and oxygen mask with soft chamois, ensuring tight fit and added comfort, plus additional safety in event of cockpit explosion. Rubber tends to vulcanize to one's hide. Sewed up my moccasins with parachute thread, riveted shoulder holster, and cleaned my .45.

Played four games of Casino with my good friend Gignac. Had a good dinner of Spam and sprouts buried in catchup, fixed my guitar, drank a bottle of port wine, contributed four shillings to the jackpot in the slot-machine. Played a few records and listened to a Nazi newscast. Plus the regular flying schedule.

Our job is defensive rather than offensive. Stick close to the Forts and scare Jerry fighters away, and can't leave the bombers we escort to give chase. Helluva note, too. D'ruther go out on low-level offensive sweeps, buzzing, hedgehopping, and shooting up enemy material, troops, trucks, barges, factories, aerodromes, etc. That sort of work is now being given to Mustang and Spit outfits. Sad, but I think we'll have a chance to mix it up royally, one day.

No haircut in several months and look a wild man. Feel like one, too. Wow. Got big rats around here. One of 'em killed our cat, Turbo, the other day. Rough situation.

Flew a little British training plane called a Gypsy Moth today. Small open-cockpit biplane and much fun for stunts. It flies good upside-down. I love to fly upside-down, for some reason.

Ol' Bottle-Arse Northrop, from Clay Center, Nebraska, wrote home a while back. A long and vivid description of life in England. Many tall stories and exaggerated experiences, etc. Well, today he gets the hometown newspaper. Since Bottle is up flying, we open up his paper and there on the front page is headline:

"LT. LEO NORTHROP IN ENGLAND!" And his letter printed verba-

Ted and his flight mates teased Leo Northrop for his quiet and fussy demeanor
as well as his weight and eating habits. Northrop always seemed to be able to
generate a meal out of nowhere, and was known to hide food in his bed.

tim below. We read it with relish, add a note or two, and install it on bulletin
board. Leo liked to've blown a gasket. Madder'n hell, and he's taken an
awful ride ever since.

Sept. 9, '43
Many thanks for pictures of me little knefyew: Andy, wonder child of the
clan. He looks to be a sharp little jerk, and I bet he finds a bit of mischief
to get into. When he runs outta ideas, I personally will tutor him. Best I
check him out in a Cub one day.

    Times is boomin' in this neck of the woods. Spent a good part of this
lovely autumn day six miles or so out of this world. Away up thar a-drivin'
around with a big hunk of machinery strapped to my behind. 'Twas a fine
sight below, with a deck of clouds away down at ten thousand feet or so,
and the bright sunshine on 'em. The map of England spread out like a big
puzzle, and the North Sea on one hand and the Channel on the other,
sparkling real purty.

    There is a couple of ARC dames stationed here. A couple of high sassiety broads from the States who are good lookin' and know it. This one blonde wench has, of late, been wearin' her hair in pigtails and runnin' around in sloppy collich fashions, etc., leading a few of the ranking officers a merry chase. Anyway, today she cruises into our officer's mess hall and sits down at the CO's table as usual, and she eats her lunch, lookin' fashionably sloppy. Well, who should walk in with the Colonel but our ol' friend Captain Clark Gable! And sits next to this blonde, who all but swoons, and we kin plainly see that this unfortunate critter wishes she were a leetle more glamorous in appearance. We sure get a bang outta little things like that. Ho! It would appear that Clark is out making the rounds of fighter bases and he has a Flying Fort with him today, with camera equipment. Our outfit has been selected to put on a show for these movies (publicity purposes, I guess) so after lunch we fly a 36-ship formation up over the clouds alongside this B-17 and they shoot pichers of us. Gable signs our short-snorters and appears to be quite a busy gent over here.

And then there was the Jerry who got blasted in the Berlin Blitz. His rescuers were guided on their way by hysterical laughter as they dug thru the debris. They finally uncover the little guy, still laughing irrationally: "You know fellows," he sez, "the funniest thing happened—I was just sitting there and I pulled this chain and the whole damn building fell down on top of me . . ."

Got to pondering today upon the many things I wear when flying. Like an old tinker who has lost his mule and must carry everything on his own back. On my head a leather helmet, lined with soft chamois: RAF issue and better than AAF stuff. In each ear there is a big earphone, and a wire runs across the back of my head connecting my ears. Only thing keeps 'em on. Big set of goggles over my eyes. Over nose and cheeks, chin and mouth is strapped a rubber oxygen mask with a hose like an elephant's trunk dangling off my snout and clamped onto my chute and connected to the oxygen-regulator at the side of my cockpit. A tiny microphone is built into the mask and sits a half-inch from my lips. A long electric cord also dangles out the front of the mask and one branch of it plugs into my helmet earphones so I kin hear the music. The other end of the cord snarls around and ends up plugged into the radio box. So much for what I wear upon my addled head.

Wear a flying suit with pockets all over the thing, in which to stick gum, maps, whiskey, cigarettes, etc. Wear a leather jacket over the suit. Wear my chute over the jacket. This chute is a very handy article. To serve as a cushion insulating my bony tail from the hard bucket seat are yards and yards of fine white silk crammed into a small package. This silkpack is topped by a rubber air cushion. The chute is held to me by maze of wide straps and buckles. The back part of the chute is a most remarkable cushion, for with the pull of a single cord it opens revealing a sizeable rubber boat complete with paddles, food, anchor, sail, mast, bailing bucket, bullet-hole plugs, fishing tackle, etc. Travel a bit farther around the chute harness and find a little packet tied on: open this out pops a tourniquet, morphine, medicine, etc.

Continue the trip, and another package built into the harness gives out with an escape-kit: maps and tiny compasses and foreign dough, water bottle, food, saws, files, and secret stuff. All the above junk is neatly stowed away about my person. Under one arm in a shoulder holster rests a .45 and on my belt is hung a razor-sharp hunting knife, used to cut parachute shroud lines in the event of a water landing. On the lapel of my jacket hangs a shiny whistle to signal passing bateaus, if ever I should find myself drifting thru a Channel fog in my rubber dinghy. Forgot to mention that over my jacket and under my chute is worn a Mae West life vest, complete with CO_2 cartridge for automatic inflation.

That takes care, roughly, of what I wear on me head and around me carcass. In a knee pocket is a little hi-pressure oxygen flask for high-altitude bail-out purposes. On me feet are me trusty moccasins. Wot a rig to be wearin' around! And overall this mess of trinkets run wires and tubes and connections plugging me into the electrical system of the ship. And over all *this* run the straps that make me a solid part of the P-47 . . . one wide strap over each shoulder holding me tight against the back of the seat and close against the armor plate. These straps run over my shoulders and down to me lap, there fastening onto my safety belt, which in turn, holds me down as tight as if I were bolted to the floor. Whee. Upside down and backwards, or rightside up feels all the same.

And with this animated rummage sale along with me, I gotta navigate, fly, aim, and shoot eight machine-guns, trip bombs, tinker eight hundred and ten gadgets, talk over the radio, listen over the radio, fly at nine hundred and four mph in the midst of six hundred and one other similar flying machines, watching out that I don't clip one of 'em and watching out that one of 'em doesn't clip me, follow instructions, use my own initiative, etc., and keep scouring the skies for some fathead in a 109. All this at one and the same time. Me achin' back. But all this excludes the possibility of us runnin' into a scrap, wherein a whole new set of rules applies, indeed. Gee, we have fun.

But what I like is to land and taxi up to the line and have a swarm of eager mechanics, technicians, radio men, prop men, engine men, gas men, oil men, intelligence officers, etc. leap upon the ship like mad. Refuel it, swab oil off 'n the windshield, rearm it, and always one of 'em whips open the canopy and sticks the Form 1 (paperwork) in my hand. Then I disconnect me: pull out plugs, unhook hooks, unsnarl straps, and then haul my frame outta the cockpit. Bum a smoke from one and a light off another and tell 'em a pack of lies. Ho ho ho.

By connecting up some of my rambling letters, like this jumble of chatter, mebbe you can get an idea of the life we lead.

Italy folded up like a punctured balloon today, I just heard. Somebody just drifted in and said so, anyway. I imagine that you at home follow the war news closer than we do. We are too busy puttering around in our own little sphere of operations. I know wots cooking over here, but I can't say, because it's a seeeecret. Mark me words, tho, there'll be plenty of flyin' for Unka Ted, and purty durn soon.

Bum joor.

Sept. 10, '43

Rained hard this day, so nothing much was on the fire. Just laid around and went to a few lectures and puttered around the pilot's ready-room basking in front of the fireplace . . . talking flying and reading combat reports and tech orders, etc. And tonight there's little to do but sit down and write another windy letter. But of late there's been quite a bit to do in the way of sitting behind a shiny twelve-foot propeller. Not so long ago was looking over the wingtip down into some six miles of thin air, and the scenery was most interesting, being as how most of this scenery belongs temporarily to A. Hitler & Co. Got a wonderful birds-eye view of the Netherlands and Belgium and a hunk of France. Have been on a few missions lately that we fondly call "rodeos" . . . a rodeo being an aerial counterpart to our South Dakota "Days of 76." Have felt 700% more eager since we started getting into trouble. And furthermore, yesterday I discarded those corroded old gold bars on my collar for some shiney new silver bars. A year of that old shavetail crap was enuf. Joe and Leo and Mac and me and a few more got our promotions together, which called for a bit of a celebration in the bar last night. Whew.

Sept. 15, '43
Been exceedingly busy of late and bushed by nightfall . . . Yesterday and today have flown three combat missions, all at very high altitude, and that hi-level stuff sure makes me sleepy. Have seen some sights that sure defy description . . . flew over the top of a big old nimbus cloud formation (those big anvil-shaped thunderheads like you see over the mountains in the States) just at sunset the other day.

The tops of these thunderheads were at 30,000 feet, and we nuzzled around the fringes and then climbed up over and she was a-boilin' bunch of soup just beneath us. This terrific cloud formation seemed to stretch from the ground clear on up to where we were thrashin' around up near the Pearly Gate somewhere. And they were gold color on the sunny side, and black as a dark hole on the other, and I could look over the steep sides of these towering clouds down onto the sprawling countryside of Belgium and France, and on one side of that wall of cloud it was already nighttime for the citizens below, for the black shadow covered the earth as far as the far horizons. It seemed symbolic, that shadow, of the Nazi occupation. Black shadow of evil over the land, or some such idea. And off the other wingtip, on the sunny side, lay the narrow end of the North Sea and the Channel, half covered with a low bank of misty clouds, and the sun shone across the water pretty as hell.

And today had a good tour over England at low level with a bunch of the boys. By golly, I got to thinkin': there I sat with the green hills and forests and rivers rolling by under my wings at 250 mph or so . . . crossed the whole of England in short order; and back in ye olden days of Robin Hood & Co. they used to gallop madly all day long, end up twenty miles from where they'd begin. How about that? Today also looked down upon Gay Paree and wondered how they were makin' out down there. Right over the territory where the swastika rules the roost. They took a good pasting today. We covered the bombers for a spell and some P-47 outfit tangled with the "Abbeville Toughs" (which is Goering's crack flying circus, made up of a bunch of yellow-nosed FW-190s.) Our outfit was too low on gas to play.

Must be very healthy, for I notice no hi-altitude effects at all. Unusual, for funny things occur up there . . . such low pressure. One swells up like a balloon. Belly, tissues, glands, all that stuff expands greatly, resulting in amusing and amazing reactions. But the tactical advantages gained by hi-altitude are well worth the physical discomfort involved.

Letters from a few of the old friends: Tommy glows over his new wings; Russ Craig clobbers the Wops with his B-26 down in Africa; Tex Gallimore dumps bombs onto the Japs down in Burma or somewhere from his B-25. All the boys is havin' a field day.

Big shindig goin' on downstairs tonight, which I will latch onto shortly. The Doc lined up a bunch of Army nurses for a dance tonight and the noise is provided by a four-piece GI band. Wheee.

Looks as if Italy is a bit tougher than expected. Wonder if the Nazi's did salvage Mussolini as is reported. Damn clever trick, if true.

Good weather fast fading. Means laying around in the fogs or auguring about within them. I don't relish either thought.

Sept. 18, '43

A beautiful day in Merrie Olde England. You bet. No great news to orate about, so will merely fill the sheet with idle thots. Today nothing wuz cooking in line of duty, probably because there wasn't a cloud in the damned sky . . . Skys were blue (and friends were true, take me back etc.)—and you oughta hear me grind that one out on the old gittar. And sing? Boy, kin I sing. Of late we outlaws have gotten together in the evenings and held sessions of delightful music. My gittar . . . Northrop twanging away on a Jews-harp . . . McKibben and Rocky and Gerst and Franky Green forming a real good barbershop quartet (emphasis on the quart). We send ourselves. Now and then the Major—Luther Richmond, our CO—drops by with his harmonicy and adds to the general uproar. The major hails from Texas and knows fifty-three verses to "'Ol Chisolm Trail," of which fifty ain't fit to print. You know how that one goes . . . sing a verse alone and then everyone in earshot chips in on the "Come a ty yi yipee yipee yow yippee yow, come a ty yi yippee yippee yay" part.

Flown some mighty interesting missions lately, and we've covered the coast of Europe from the Frisian Islands up beyond the Zuider Zee to the other side of Le Havre quite thoroughly. Got near to Paris covering a bomber expedition not long ago. Spectacular to see those big babies plowing steadily along thru the flak in their tight box formation, with all of us jerks whippin' around over 'em in an effort to keep enemy fighters from interfering with proceedings. The Forts sure like to see us around when they're over Occupied country. Matter of fact, I met a couple of Fortress jockeys in London, and they fetched me a tall drink when they found I was a peashooter.

Say, we had a gay party the other night. The sawbones imported a flock of Army nurses which turned out that they wuz drafted in the last war, or the one before. Spanish-American vets, I'd judge. So the boys and me drink the punch and retire to have a poker game.

Ain't seen any of them there leetle gremlins lately. These English gremlins are naturally quite reserved and not at all rambunctious like their pale-face brothers across the Great Water. First one of these Limey gremlins I see I'm gonna let fly with me trusty .45. Must be constant breathing of pure oxygen that results in my capricious moods, like this.

Christmas shopping. A matter I've been pondering. Nothing in London. Shops are bare. You folks don't have to worry about me. Send me a good pocket-knife, as mine disintegrated the other day. Another small job I'd like is a silver flask, for booze, to carry tucked into my flying suit somewhere in case of sometime I might float around the Channel in a rubber dinghy for a few cold days. In that case, I might as well enjoy meself.

Of recent days have had a turrible crave for a shrimp cocktail. We have a fairly steady diet of Spam and stuff like that there, and when I see a plateful of Spam I go into a trance and before my eyes appears a shrimp cocktail, so then I eat fast before it goes away. Get good breakfasts and a couple of really good lunches a week.

Mashed pertaters sometimes, and corn. Suppers are pretty good except for the fact that we gotta wear blouses in order to eat. Dumbest damn thing I ever herd of. Bassards in London HQ thought that 'un up. That's all they got to do. Bassards sit around town and plot and plan and wait til a good foggy day and send us out on some hare-brained expedition, then they tell us we gotta wear blouses to chow. Never heard of such dumb types.

Get two days off every ten days and can't fly on our days off. New rule the boss put in because we wuz all hangin' around moaning and trying to get on a milk-run mission when we wuz supposed to be relaxing somewhere. If that two days off is relaxation, then somebody better dig out his dictionary.

If someday you decide you want to go abroad and see England, well, stay to home because we got it beat by a long shot. Around here in the country it looks exactly like southern Minnesota . . . same trees and same creeks and same rollin' hills. But these folks are behind us by about sixty years in most things: like sanitation and health measures. They never heard of testing dairy cows for TB over here. Farming methods are obsolete, and I do believe their way of thinking has been in a rut since the Romans took outta here. No like to live here. Mess of historical ruins and so forth scattered around. Towns are a maze of narrow, crooked alleys with rows of beat-up old houses leaning over into the street. What they need is some good sharp promoting. After the war I'll clean up sellin' 'em man-sized cars and shower baths and neon signs and budweiser beer and rye-whisky. I'll institute dollars and cents and give pounds and shillings back to the Indians. I'll cut the cables on all the barrage balloons and let the cockeyed island sink (rumor has is that they are all that hold the place up.) After that chore is done, I'll go home and annex Canada onto the USA and chop it up into a couple of States and name one after myself.

That latter project will take some assistance, probably, but I know where to the find the boys who will do 'er.

Sept. 19, '43
Everybody happy? If not, there ain't no reason not to be. Take it from me. I spread cheer and laughter tonight. It don't cost much more to go first-class, and if that philosophy won't do the trick, I advise you get busy and make funny faces at yourself in a mirror. Ho ho ho. I hollers right and left, ho ho ho. Comes bad weather like today and all day long I prance hither and yon up and down the line of our planes where the mechanics toil and cuss and fix and smoke and spit and moan and polish and sometimes tend to become baffled by their work. From ship to ship I hop, and back to mine, shooting the breeze and swapping lies and bumming smokes and lending a palsied hand here and there, and in general violating all the non-fraternizing traditions of the Army. But I have the sweetest-running engine and the highest polish on my wings, and my crew laughs with glee at my oldest and corniest jokes. Method in me madness. Things running smoothly, and we get a lot of fun out of life. In a mischievous mood the other night and full of scotch, I type off a dandy new set of flying regulations and poop with sarcastic cracks thinly veiled in a foolish, official

patter. The Big Wheel gets ahold of it and it is fortunate that he is equipped with a sense of humor. He got a big charge out of it, and me too . . . We've got a couple of Irish Setter pups down in the lounge tonight and they're the center of attention.

Have extended my first-hand knowledge of geography lately to cover that part of France south and west of the Isles of Jersey and Guernsey. Know where the town of Nantes is? Been there. Didn't exactly poke thru town, but whizzed over it at some 400 mph, so can't tell you much about it. When my granchilluns asks me, "Hey grandaddy, wuz youse ever dere in dis here town Paris huh?" why, I kin honestly say, "Why nacherly, Rover . . . yore ol' granddaddy wuz everywhere." And then I will draw upon my wicked imagination and commence to spin the rascals stories that'll make their ears twitch and they'll run from the room looking for their maw who will wash out their little mouths with soap if they try to tell her what "Grandddaddy sez it's so, mama!"

I'll be forced to use fanciful lies when orating about them furrin towns, because you don't see a helluva lot of the homelife and shops and statues of nobility when you careen by them at some five miles per minute. Also there ain't much time to ponder the historical background of, say, Brussels, when you are trying to look behind you and in front of you at the same time. (Look in front for somebody to go hunting at, and look behind for somebody who is going hunting at you. Etc.) One of my secret ambitions is to slip "Wabash Cannonball" into the philharmonic musician's score.

Saw a powerful good movie tonight . . . "Commando's Strike at Dawn." Guys shooting guys with arrers and cuttin' throats, etc. Peachy. Before the show we had a half-hour of aircraft recognition movies. They always slip us a mickey like that . . . here we thot we wuz thru with the day's business.

Tuned in the radio in the pilot's hut today and got to tinkering around with short-wave and picked up Java. A Jap news commentator speaking singsong English. Wot a pack of lies. Wait til we get to flying against those baboons. We reached the bloodthirsty decision over a case of Ale that, when we'd driven those animals back to Japan, we'd like to round 'em up. Males females and pups, form them up in a column of twos and march the whole gibbering lot of 'em up the slope of Fujiama and off the lip of the crater and into the bubbling vat of lava below. There'll come the day when they pay for Bataan, etc.

I find right now a couple of the boys sitting here flapping their jaws and wondering what they're gonna do for excitement after the war: a novel idea comes out of this discussion. We catch a boat for South America and get a suite of rooms in a hotel high in the Andes mountains . . . Then on a dark and stormy night we will sneak like Indians to the border between Peru and Equador and move the boundary stakes over, one way or the other, about two feet. Then we retire to our suites and await developments, in the gay company of senoritas and tall, cool drinks. Within the week there will be a war or revolution and then we kin get good jobs flying for somebody.

While our big bombers were pounding Rome not so long ago, an amusing scene took place in one of those bombers. Right after the bombardier let fly with his eggs, a sergeant gunner picked up a violin he'd smuggled aboard and began to fiddle like mad. Emulating Nero. Now I wonder how long this gunner had nurtured that goddam idea?

Now I gotta go to bed, but hate to. Always feel best late at night. Mental activity perks up when the sun goes down. Understand it wuz the same with Jesse James. He done all his dirty work by night. Guess I'll sneak off to the kitchen and cut me a big hunk of cold turkey (Spam-type.) Time's a-wastin'!

Sept. 29, '43

Doggoned if I know where the days go. Go past like a string of Thunderbolts flying in trail, which is fast. Not a great deal to chatter about, but as usual I'll end up with three or four pages of odds and ends.

Enclosed find stuff clipped from our daily scandal sheet, *Stars and Stripes*. Gives you a rough idea of the rodeo show that's going on in this neck of the woods. From your Chicago papers you probably get a business-like and somewhat dry impression of our proceedings. But from the cockpit right in the cockeyed thunder of this deal, I can naturally peek into the human and intriguing angles. For example, I can see the complicated planning behind one of these escorted bomber raids—and there is planning a-plenty. Try to feature four or five big bomber squadrons and eight or ten fighter outfits scattered all over the eastern edge of England. They all take off at different times, bombers first, for they're slower. They fly different speeds on different courses for different distances. Then just before our bombers arrive over dangerous territory, they're met by a bunch of these here '47s, who escort 'em a while inland. Course is changed a few times, maybe. Then at a certain time and place, another bunch of fighters arrives and takes over the escort job, to protect the bombers over their target and partway out again. Then a third or fourth gang of fighters makes rendezvous and takes the big friends home. The above is the theory of an escorted raid. But figger an eager pilot in each separate fighter, hoping that a Jerry fighter squadron will attack the bombers, and figure a wary crew in each of our bombers hoping that nuthin' like that will happen, and you've got some story. It's some sight to see. Big boxes of bombers heading relentlessly for their target. Occasional smudges of flak in amongst 'em. Below them, maybe some scattered clouds, and below the clouds the peaceful-looking countryside of France or Belgium or Holland flows by.

And up where we are, a restless crew of fighter pilots twisting and turning back and forth across the bombers' line of flight. Each pilot has a definite hunk of sky to search with his eyes, plus each pilot naturally looking after his own hide, whether or not he's supposed to. Especially, we focus our glazed eyeballs into the sun and around behind us, for that's where Jerry lurks. Each guy hopes he'll be first to spot enemy aircraft, and the one who does calls it in over the radio. Everybody—bomber to bomber, fighter-to-fighter, and bomber-to-fighter—is connected by radio, and since the Jerries listen in on all our chatter, serious talk is done in code words.

All of which is a sketchy picture of one small part of a bomber-escort mission. Can't concentrate on giving a clearer picture, for right around me are four and twenty throttle-jockeys discussing everything but business at the top of their lungs. I recall that back in the States, it was only a few of the lads wanted to get into fighters. Flying bombers was the great thing. I know when I was in Basic Flying School at Minter Field, only six of us out of a class of some two hundred demanded, insisted, and threatened to retire if we weren't given fighter training . . . The rest all figured to live long, take a soft job flying a nice, big, safe twenty-five engine bomber. But now lookit. Ho ho ho ho!

I send a clipping concerning this yellow-nosed bunch of Jerry fighter pilots. Those jerks'll wish they were honest fishermen when we get our sights on 'em.

A letter from Russ Craig from North Africa. He's flying a durned good ship and is evidently getting all the action he wants. Would be willing, however, to give Africa back to the cannibals or whatever the hell lives there. I was lucky to be stationed in England, for here we live the gay life in our spare time. Just hop into the cockpit, careen around uncivilized skies for a while, and then land back home again, stepping out back into luxury, comfort, and within range of queens and good whisky. I reiterate: wot a way to run a war.

Chapter 5

Review of England

October 2, '43

Monotonous times of late. A week of foul weather and all is grounded. But it's clearing now, and tomorrow should be flying again. Right now the sun is out and things look pretty as can be. The leaves are turning color now, and it won't be long until that long and miserable winter sets in. A lot of flying then in ugly weather. Gets dark now by seven in the evening, and soon it'll be blackout-time by four in the afternoon. The land of the foggy, long nights.

Enclosed find pictures. That character in the cockpit is the leader of that famed flying circus renowned throughout ETO fighter circles. I chuckle. Next one I have taken I will wear my oxygen mask and goggles pulled down so no one will again be exposed to that leer. Am also without Mae West in this picture. (Mae West being a life vest, drat it.) Up inside the windshield you kin see a wee bit of the gunsight. And up top is the rear-vision mirror. Those bulging ears are result of the RAF-type helmet. Behind me is a crash pad mounted on a slab of armor plate. They pay me about $300 per month to drive this critter. Ho ho! Somebody's gettin' robbed and it ain't me.

At this point I'm a settin' by a large open window. Cool breezes float in. Green meadow sprawled out for a quarter mile. Big grove of chestnut trees sprouting off to one side. Little bunnies hoppin' to and fro and chasing each other in circles, with what in mind we all know, knowing bunnies. Gray and white clouds breaking up now to let the sunshine through in nice slanting columns. Little doghouse parked below the window with three two-week-old cocker spaniels playin' together. One of the boys just cruised in with a large rabbit-burger in his hand. He sez in a profound voice: "Wot a way to run a war!" I sez, sure as hell, Jack. Sherman was so right.

But tomorrow we ought to have a good mission lined up. Hope we escort again. We like to do that because then there is more chance that we'll meet up with some varmint to swap lead with. Reach fer yore hawg-laig, strangeh . . . bam bam . . . smile when you say that, pardner . . . bam bam . . . (Sound effects of bottles crashing and furniture busting . . . then another bam bam and a window tinkles to bits . . . then the sound of the Faro Kid galloping away on his 2,000 horses!) Dunno how that snuck into this epic of the stratosphere (lookit that last word, willya!) You kin tell how I've been spending the day. And that tangent I just got off on sounds just like one of our party's.

Anyway, this zero-zero ain't good. How we gonna ruin the Luftwaffe if we can't get offa the ground?

Having no war-stories to tell about, I'll light into England for a change. This country is backward. Highways and hotels are both lousy. Telephone service is worse than our rural turn-the crank stuff. Their ideal of something fancy in the line of sewage disposal, or whatever you call it, is a roofless outhouse with nothin' to sit on inside. Go into the kitchen of any restaurant in Cambridge or Norwich and all but the finest in London, and you'll walk over grease and soot and filth of two-hundred and seventeen years of cooking. Cooks, waiters, and cashiers with grimy hands and cruddy aprons. And the pubs, which correspond with our taverns and beer joints, are the prize of the lot. Can smell 'em clear down the block—handy in fog or blackout, however, as one can come in on the beam. Dark and dimly lit they are, with streaked walls and mirrors opaque with good ol' dirt. The bar will be sticky with a week's spillings, and the technique for pouring a glass of ale is this: the lousy old bottle is upended into the glass and the ale bubbles forth and rises up over the bottle and the thumb and first three fingers of the innkeeper. Neatly done. The barkeep is a character in himself. In the smaller pubs he generally looks like a W. Madison street bum, dressed up somewhat. Wash their mitts upon retiring. In the famous Liverpool St. Station, with terrific volume of traffic, there is a bar, but not like even one of our wee saloons, this one has a distinctive odor and within you will see three old and garrulous barmaids of a type one might find swamping out an office building at five a.m. They run the joint. Fat, greasy hands, black fingernails, and sweat-soaked dresses. They peddle the bitters: a swish of a dirty glass thru a pan of greasy water and it's set for the next customer. Boy, you don't know just how clean we are back home.

And once in a while some jerk over here makes it clear that we're just tolerated as a necessary evil towards finishing up the war. And many an operator will adjust his prices as high as he thinks the traffic will bear. An evening in a London nightclub might run a hundred bucks for a pair of Yank flyers, whereas the same affair would only nick a pair of Englishmen a third of that. But what the hell, we throw our dough around when on leave, and one can expect a gouge now and then. Only it ain't done with finesse, as is the case in NYC. Characters running clubs run pretty true to form, here and there.

I think after the war there'd be a little unrest here, for we've treated one and all with complete equality, and some here find our friendliness hard to savvy. I think we're educating 'em a little in the ways of democracy. Some of these downtrodden worker types tend to greet us with low bows, but we don't like that sort of carrying on, and when we let 'em know, they come on up and greet us with open arms. When the Americans go back home, some of these guys aren't going to like having to bow and scrape again. There must be a general lack of education for one and all over here. Maybe that accounts for the backwardness of the whole country. If the next generation would get to thinking and analyzing and comparing their standard of living with ours, then would come the revolution, for they wouldn't stand for an antiquated way of living when there was a modern, healthier way within reach. They need some ideas.

You know the average American in this war has the idea that an Englishman is a cool customer who putters about in the ruins of his home picking up bits of wife and kiddies without cracking a smile. But I think we can go further. Habit's got 'em by the nose. If while examining a leg of his smallest child, this Englishman should discover that it was eleven a.m., he would drop the leg and make for the nearest Tea Shoppe. But it's true that they have guts, and the more they're bombed, the more resolute to fight they become. But then again, I suppose that's true of the Norwegians, Czechs, Poles . . . or for that matter, the Jerries may be facing our ruthless bombings with a good deal of fortitude. I for one hope not (the latter case). Hope they're terrified.

After the war, tho, when the English get a chance to turn their efforts into channels other than war production, they'll probably run a lot of improvements. They'll have to if they expect to keep up with things. Maybe they'll even give us Canada in payment of debts incurred during several wars. Who kin tell?

Chapter 6

....

Back to the Nissen

Oct. 9, '43

Just back from London and a two-day leave. Fine time, and took in a couple of shows. Also got an eyeful of a flock of Jerry planes scouring around overhead last night. Biggest air raid on London in a long while. Interesting. They didn't hit any special target . . . just bombed here and there. A bunch of searchlights would catch a ship in their cone of light and then the flak would sail up and bust all around 'em. Couple of ships came streaking down and did more damage when they hit than their bombs. Ol' Frank Greene and I hear all the sireeens a-howlin' and we order up another scotch-and-soda and wander outside to take a look. Flak clatters and clanks all around in the streets and perforates the rooftops. Ruddy glare lights up the clouds when a good fire gets going over near the docks. Helluva sight, and if people hadn't been getting killed and houses getting burned, I'd liked to have watched it longer. Also swapped lies with a couple of war correspondents.

Was due back at the field at noon yesterday but the engine on this slick little toonerville-type milk train busted down and we sat on a siding outside of Cambridge for a few hours. We got back just in time to watch the squadron take off on a choice mission. Hate to miss out on any fun. However, today is bright and clear and cold so I'm waiting for the good word on today's flying. Think today it'll be fur jacket and boots. You know, the outside air temperature at thirty-thousand feet is generally down around forty or fifty below zero. Chilly. Not bad at all in the cockpit, though, for there

59

I'm parked right behind a couple thousand horsepower and she throws off a lot of heat. Have a heater, too. A long, flexible tube that spouts hot air. Can steer it around and clear up places on the canopy or windshield that might ice up. Generally stick it down first one boot and then the other.

Say, I neglect to say that we've moved out of our castle and back into that quaint ol' corrugated tin Nissen hut. Matter of fact, I like it better. C-flight lives together again: Gerst, Rauk, Green, McKibben, Northrop, Heller, MacKean, and me. A little bit chilly sleeping these nights, but I don't t mind that. It might be tents such as our mechanics live in. I haven't had my long-johns off, day or night, for some time now, and to keep my bean warm I wear at night a wool knit job that is quite the thing. Every time I put it on, my good friend Mac goes into hysterical laughter. Hell, I don't see anything so funny about wearing a hat to bed if your head gets

352nd men lounging outside their Nissen hut, with friend.

cold. This morning at four a.m. I awoke to hear fleet after fleet of our bombers forming up overhead, which means we go out pretty soon. Mechanics preflighting our ships somewhere out in the cold sunrise. Sounds mighty nice, those engines.

Oct. 10, '43

Went in a long way today on escort. En route, climbing for altitude and heading for Holland, received some very interesting information over the radio. You know, our radios are on all the time we're in the air, and naturally the Jerries try to ball up our reception by a process called jamming. Today they varied their usual methods by broadcasting a shrill metallic whine, which at first varied in pitch. Then the pitch variations became words and sentences. First a whine, then words repeated monotonously like this: "Wheee wheee wheeeeeeyou're going in you're going in you're going in you won't get home you won't get home you won't get home grrr grrr grrr goering goering goering you won't get home you're going in you're in you're in you're in won't get home won't get home . . ." Then a string of words meant to add to the intended psychological effect of the foregoing, like so: "You're in you're in won't get out won't get out won't get out . . ." All this in a very shrill, high monotone.

We did indeed get in and way in over hostile country, and then on the way out the Jerrys' jamming changed into a squeaky, "I'm a hero I'm a hero I'm a hero I'm a hero . . ." (About ten minutes of that and one of the boys cuts in his mike and gives with a few insults and a raucous razz.) This type of jamming is intended to rattle us and get us jumpy, I s'pose, but we sort of enjoy it. Gives us something to listen to on an otherwise quiet radio. As for getting us rattled, those Jerry ground-hogs ought to try flying instruments in a thunderstorm sometime.

Had a good day today. An amusing habit the ground crew has: every mission calls for a new belly tank becuz we drop them off after having emptied them. So the mechanics generally scribble various tender messages on 'em. Paint their thoughts of the Nazzies in bold red letters. Bet the folks in the occupied countries who find 'em get a bang out of them. Ugly caricatures with appropriate inscriptions painted alongside. Ours today all went in the drink, however. If the one I dropped ever floats back to England, there will undoubtedly be a complaint registered by some shocked and outraged lady. And if she registers no complaint, then she ain't no lady.

Oct. 12, '43

Well, tally-hoooo! Been big game hunting again. Not so long ago, wuz churning around five or six miles up in the air a'swappin' lead with some character who was out to perforate Mac and me and our beautiful aircraft. That morning we were briefed as to our mission and warned of some new and fancy tactics to expect from the pride of the Luftwaffe. Then we slip into our duds, strapping on all sorts of awkward items: pistols, knives, dinghy boats, bundles of silk, packages of money and bandages and the damnedest assortment of junk you'll ever see. And we head for our ships on what might be called a run, but which really adds up to be a comical waddle. Mechanics greet us with a "Where ya goin', Lootenant?" and we tell 'em some tall story and snicker when we see what they've written on the belly tanks. So into the cockpit I wedge and flutter around sticking wires into my ears so I kin hear, tubes into my nose so I kin breathe, and plugs into other places so I kin talk. Adjust straps and belts and run a look over the controls and look at my watch waiting for start-engine time. I wave the boys off my wings and turn 'er over and warm up that lovely engine, give the crew the o.k. sign, and taxi out, joining a flock of other ships already on the move. Formup with Frank Green and Joe Gerst and McKibben, whose wing I am flying. So we taxi down to the takeoff funnel and off we go, lickety damn split, in a nice tight formation takeoff, four abreast we are. As usual, I have a few anxious moments here and just clear the end of the runway and drag my belly thru the treetops, weighted down with all this extra gas load. Then too, it is pretty durned foggy weather, and we lost sight of the ground as soon as we got airborne.

But soon we're up in bright sunlight and there are all those squadrons neatly formed and climbing fast towards the Channel. Pretty soon the coast of England slides away below somewhere and we head out to the Continent, climbing high toward our rendezvous point. And in several minutes we spot a whole flock of our bombers. Then we're over them and start our escort, essing back and forth over their lead formation, and keeping our bloodshot 20-20 eyes peeled for Jerry fighters who might wish to spoil the bombers' fun. Great numbers of U.S. aircraft driving deeper and deeper thru Belgium and toward the target in Germany. Get the picture? Our R.T. has been silent to this point. Now starts a little radio chatter, somewhat as follows:

"Contrails, three o'clock high!" (Contrails are cloud-tracks or vapor-trails marking the wake of high-flying ships . . .) "Got 'em spotted. Keep an eye on 'em!"

"Contrails five o'clock high! Watch 'em, gang!"

"Look like bandits!" (enemy aircraft)

"Ah, they're little friends!" (friendly aircraft)

"Don't look so goddam friendly to me!"

"Bandits six o'clock high! Watch 'em!"

"Twelve plus bandits six o'clock high! Red leader, starboard turn, ninety degrees!"

"HERE THEY COME! BREAK RIGHT, RED AND BLUE FLIGHTS!"

Me being involved in this latter command, I flick on my gun switch and Mac and I turn sharply into the oncoming Jerries, meeting their attack head on. In this set of circumstances, Mac and I become a closely cooperating team, he doing the shooting with me sticking close to him and covering his tail while he concentrates on what's ahead.

So this one Me 109 comes driving at Mac and me with his guns a' winking and blinking. At the same time Mac cuts loose with a long burst and I give a squirt, having nothing to lose by so doing. This Jerry drives past us fast and I do mean fast, for our closing speed is maybe over 700 mph. We're up around 30,000 feet, and Mac jerks back his stick and kicks rudder in an attempt to turn around and get on this bird's tail, but we overdo it and the two of us spin out, corkscrewing vertically with him looking for something to shoot at and with me craning my neck around and around to cover the sky behind us. It strikes me as being comical, this spinning in close formation, and I realize that it isn't one of the things recommended for longevity, and when Mac recovers, I recover too, automatically because I'm flying formation with him, and when he ends our vertical dive with a fleeting shot at some passing ship, he evidently gets a glimpse behind him and sees a fighter on his tail. Not realizing it's just pore ol' Ted, he cranks his tired Thunderbolt thru some very fine evasive action until I can slide out to one side so he can get a look at me. So we zoom for altitude and look around.

Perhaps twenty seconds have elapsed since the command "Break!" And where a half minute before we'd been flying along peaceably in the midst of a couple hundred friendly bombers and fighters, now we search the sky vainly for signs of a plane of any description. Absolutely nothing in sight! No one in the sky but the two of us. Which is always one of the most amazing things about this racket. One moment the sky is full of ships chasing tails and rolling and zooming and looping, and then they're completely dispersed. But where the funny part came in during our brief combat was to hear the R.T. chatter.

"Break left, Scotty!"

"Lookit that bassard go willya!"

"Blue Three, you better do something. You got a Jerry on yer tail!"

"Hit the deck, wheeeee!"

"Strikes on that S.O.B.!"

Stuff like that there, only a lot more and more profane and gleeful. But here are we a couple of hundred miles into Germany, so we pick up a heading and zigzag for home with our throttles bent clear over the stop. We give each other cross-cover and stupidly give up a chance to clobber a slow-rolling Jerry we see beneath us, figuring him to be bait. Pretty soon, landfall-in and we land with just enuf gas. Then we join the boys already home and count noses until the whole gang is together again, hashing over the day's fun. Our part of the mission was pronounced successful in that none of our bombers were bounced while we were escorting them. But Mac and I cuss ourselves for not taking that single encountered on the way home.

A lazy day, this one. Fog hangs thickly over the field. Have had several good frosts, and of late we've picked a bunch of chestnuts and roasted 'em on the stove-top in our hut . . . hi ho.

Oct. 13, '43

Enclosed find pictures of Joe and Rocky and Mac, who are three old-timers in the outfit, and the four of us are durned good friends . . . Our fighter tactics are based on the fact that two ships working together are more effective than three or four ships fighting individually. Well, over here Joe and Rocky make up one team and Mac and I make up another. Always fly together, wing to wing, and one does the shooting and the other covers. Fly together and spend leave together. Mac's a clever feller, good flyer, and has a very excellent and whimsical sense of humor indeed. Full of mischief. We get along.

. . . Another long flight today, most of it in bad weather.

Nothing much to spout about. Frank Greene and Cutler and me took a little hike yesterday and came back with a bucketful of chestnuts, which have been squirming atop the stove ever since. A lot of 'em hereabouts. Also located some black raspberry bushes loaded to the ground with big ripe berries. Stood around and et 'em til our tongues were purple. Had a peach of a feed the other night . . . pheasant and partridge dinner. Skeet guns and a deal with a local gamekeeper—a couple of pounds to the latter and he overlooks the fact that the birds we clobber are to be donated to the King. We explored a dense forest the other night by moonlight . . . huge owls flapped around and rabbits hopped out right from under our feet. And, by golly, we saw a flock of big pheasants roosting high in a big oak tree. Saw pheasants once before in trees, back in Dakota. Also found nice apple orchard!

"Here are the hot-shots what won the bloody war: C Flight of the 486th squadron. We flew together for three years. Got our wings in October '42 and fought the battle of Holyoke, New London, Farmingdale, Greenwich Village, and Kilmer before we even shipped out. Played Red-dog from NYC to Scotland, rented a private distillery, and carried on from there. Drink the Flight Surgeon out of alcohol, the pubs in 100 mile radius out of brew, raised the prices around Piccadilly Circus. Decreased the German population and increased the English population. Flew a total of around 3,000 hours combat together, too. At present, all twiddle their thumbs around the USA waiting for another war. Above, L to R: Bottle-Arse Northrup, Mac McKibben, Parchesi-Joe Gerst, Geronimo Greene, da Faro Kid (me), Robbie MacKean (KIA), and Flatfoot Heller. Below: Tex Brashear and Lloyd Archibald Rauk."

Chapter 7

Squadron Characters

Oct. 14, '43

F ew more pichers. Ugly mugs enclosed are more of the boys out of the old Fightin' 21st, and naturally my best pals becuz we hit Trumblull together last January and sweated out the hard-luck months together. Frank Greene is C-Flight leader these days. He and Northrop are leading element and Mac and I the second pair. Frank's allright, and we've followed him thru thick and thin. He and I just spent a colossal two days in London. Happy-go-lucky sort of guy, and another with a quaintly distorted sense of humor. Frank Cutler's a reckless gent. Excellent flyer and loves death and destruction, same like the rest of us. A vicious temper at times, and at others, a sentimental, philosophical gent. Loves the country as I do and we often wander around, poking thru the woods and admiring the beauty of things in general. His young brother was killed recently flying in Texas as a Navy cadet. Capt. Eddie Gignac looks like a pirate in this picture, but I think he's the best-liked feller in the squadron. A little short stocky guy, face scarred up from a deal in which he was knocked down by Japs in the Pacific. Crashed in jungles and fished out by natives after a week or so. Pappy was intercollegiate nat'l. ski-jumping champ a few years ago. Holds the Silver Star for gallantry. He's the funniest guy I ever knew . . . a born comedian, and hope you can meet him some day. A wild man in an airplane . . . unpredictable violent maneuvers. I know, for I've flown alongside a few rounds.

Been flying different ships of late and wish I'd get another of my own. All a bit different. Temperamental things they are, just like you dames.

Oct. 17, '43

Letter from Tommy Price, who is following in my footsteps, for he's up at Westover flying '47s. He writes an exuberant letter and when I write him back he's due for a terrific blow to his pride and morale. Not only is ol' Tom following my tracks in line of aircraft, but he also mentions a certain off-duty cutey with whom I have had a nodding acquaintance. Ha ha ha! But don't think Tom'll have to loaf around up there. Our outfit was more or less a guinea-pig deal, and things are getting organized these days as regards Thunderbolts.

Pretty bad weather of late. Fog and rain and low cloud. Flew a mission yesterday and ended up coming back alone. Flew as spare pilot and accompanied the squadron clear to Belgium waiting for someone to drop out

Ted, Frank Cutler, and Frankie Greene. Of Frank Cutler, Ted says: "Killer Cutler, he was known as, and with just reason, for anything that moved when he was aloft soon was shot full of 50-caliber holes. Frank is one of the hottest pilots in the group. Perfect temperament for fightin' and flyin'. But he met a Jerry FW-190 jockey who was as ornery as himself. In a dogfight, Frank made a head-on attack, shooting all the way in and trying to make his opponent give way first. But neither ship changed course and they met head-on, disappearing in a cloud of spare parts."

and leave a hole for me to fill. But no squadron engine, oxygen, or radio trouble, so had to turn tail and skeedaddle for home. But had a lot of fun en route, for I was laying beautiful contrails behind me and I could look into my mirror and watch 'em roll out like smoke out of a sky-writer ship. So I proceeded to loop and roll and barrel-roll all the way downhill till finally I hit the coast of England, where I found a mass of low clouds completely covering the land. So went out to sea a little ways and flew along the front looking for a hole to enter, and found a nice little tunnel into which I headed at a slow 250 mph. Delightful it was to see all the fantastic cloud shapes and forms loom up. Some of 'em I'd dodge and others I'd plunge into, going on instruments for a while. Got darker and darker and finally I went over to instrument flying and let down to 300 feet and could then make out ground beneath me. So hedge-hopped all the way home and landed only because I was low on gas.

Raining hard now, and not a thing in the line of business. The fire is stoked with a couple chunks of wood and there is a poker game in the offing, I fear. For Rocky is collecting a big pile of English pennies which we use for poker chips at a shilling each. The doc just came in and is spraying noses right and left. We've all had slight colds for a week or so, but flying at altitude hasn't bothered me a great deal, oddly enuf. Matter of fact, I think that those constant pressure changes do a lot of good towards clearing up bad sinus conditions.

Inasmuch as the poker game is stalled for a while, here are some more of my pilot pals in this here outfit. Here's Ed Heller, and his name fits. Biggest gent in the squadron, maybe 200 pounds and six foot tall. Ex-Pennsylvania State Trooper and nicknamed, nacherly, Flatfoot. A hot pilot, and we argue now and then that his flying is no brain and all muscle, strictly, as compared with mine being a case of mind over matter. Powerful big guy and has the heartiest belly-laugh I ever heard. Good friend. Picture here also of Scotty, me ol' pal indeed. A cagey Scot he is. Leo Northrop is a character. Prima-donna type of the outfit, and we humor him to keep him happy at times, and at others, a little needling results in a condition of pompous indignation. He's a good type, and just wait till Clay Center, Nebraska gets him back. Corky Corcoran's a peach of a guy. Great tall lanky bag of bones and another good pilot. Subtle humor, and the only one of the more reckless bunch who's married. All the foregoing gents are in this racket for love of it, and each considers the war as a lovely opportunity for legalized buzzing in the finest available equipment. About half of the rest of the squadron pilots are married, I guess, and that fact seems to inject a dose of caution into their flying. It's the footloose and fancy-free individualist who makes for good fighter-pilot material.

Had a fire in our pilots' hut the other night and the joint burned down, but we salvaged all flying equipment but lost all our girlie-type etchings. A pity. Well, the fire's going good and the roof ain't leakin' too much and we outghta be real happy, but you've never seen abject misery until you've seen a gang of grounded fighter-pilots. One day we started cutting out paper dolls and stringing 'em from one end of the hut to the other.

The Doc is done and the poker game is calling.

Oct. 20, '43

More characters in this noble organization: Don Higgins, who evidently lives on borrowed time. Bailed out of his '47 back in the States from low level and his chute just popped when his feet hit the ground. Lit a few feet away from the hole his ship dug when it augured in. Ship hit in a frozen lake and blasted a small turtle out of his hibernating place in the mud. We kept the turtle around for a mascot, flew with it, logged it's time, let it swim in champagne, and it finally died when somebody left it overnight in a tin-cup of whiskey. This Higgins also walked away from a spectacular crash with just a wee cut on an arm. Flew thru a grove of ancient oaks.

Miklajcyk (Black Mike), a screwball professional aviator. Our engineering officer as well as excellent combat pilot. Lives, breathes, and talks nothing but flying, and is delighted to be over here chasing around the stratosphere in a hot ship.

Al Marshall was, I think, a law student before the war. Fine conversationalist and loves to argue, which he does with high logic and driving home his points with triumphant smiles. Smokes a foul pipe and plays a nice piano and holds his own at the bar.

Luther Richmond flies at the front of our squadron and is responsible for a couple of million bucks worth of planes and pilots whenever we take off. He figures tactics and gives the orders over the RT. A calculating, conservative leader, knows all the angles and is decisive. Hard to know and stands off a little ways from the boys. Much time in the air from running a training-command outfit in Texas. Sometimes we wish he'd be a wee bit less conservative, for we generally chafe at the bit and would mix it up

Henry Miklajcyk was one of the most technically and tactically-minded pilots of the 486th. He scored 7.5 aerial victories before being shot down and killed on November 2, 1944. Ted calls him "Miklajcyk (Black Mike), a screwball professional aviator. Our engineering officer as well as excellent combat pilot. Lives, breathes, and talks nothing but flying, and is delighted to be over here chasing around the stratosphere in a hot ship."

sometimes regardless of odds. He's absolutely fair and square and we never underestimate him, which would be easy to do. Still water running deep applies to Luther . . .

Don't suppose people in the States realize that the second front they've been hollering for has been in operation for many months now over here. Night and day, fleets of hundreds of U.S. and RAF heavy bombers have been going deep into the heart of the olde country. There they dump their bombs and blow large chunks of Germany high into the blue. If this relentless night and day attack ain't a second front, I'd like to know what one is. (I think that this steamroller bombing expedition is paving the way for a ground invasion to take place next spring sometime.) This bombing is the ideal way to finish Germany. A good attack by a fleet of B-17s, and one less industrial section. We cut out the ball-bearing outfit at Schweinfurt with a loss of 60 bombers, more or less, which is high losses but low compared to a ground army's losses. But I think our High Command makes a mistake by not cutting power supply. They should leave the factories alone and concentrate on dams, power-stations, railroads, etc. Without coal available for the generators, the factories would soon slow down. Cut the railroad tracks and blow the dams and let a thousand 8th AF fighters work over their transportation, and more good would be done than has been done with all this hard-target bombing.

McKibben just came in from test-hopping his ship after some repairs. (Fifteen minutes ago a ship came over our hut, clearing the roof by about ten feet, with the suction about lifting the bunks off the floor. I remarks to Greene: There goes Mac . . . and naturally, it wuz him.) He comes in grinning. "Howdja like that 'un?"

Oct. 23, '43
So Len is flying bombardment, hey? Sorry he isn't flying fighters. Looks like the end of a long and beautiful friendship. They do the dirty work and we cop the sporting end of this flying war.

Been on a couple or three more of those long-range missions lately . . . went clear into the Ruhr Valley, where I guess they manufacture nothing but flak guns. So now have scanned the continent that much deeper. Yesterday wuz the deal, tho. Away we go into a foggy, hazy, cloudy, rainy, and plenty stormy-looking sky. Spend a couple of hours at altitude milling around and never did see blue sky. But despite the freezing temperature in the cockpit, was wringing wet the whole time. That's hard work, trying to maintain a decent formation when you can see no ground or sky at all. Just a gray void with all kinds of cloud forms hanging in the general haze. Mizzable thing. Finally after searching futilely for the bombers we were to've met, we dive down to ten or twelve thousand to where we can see the ground. Looked to me like England and we circled a while, found out it was Calais area and so went home to England.

Be kinda humiliating to buzz a field you thought to be friendly and get a green light from the tower and come in and set down. Then taxi up to the line and have some Jerry poke a pistol under your nose. For a fact, it's happened. It seems that once upon a time at a certain airdrome in England, and near our own, some of our fighters were expected to land after

The 486th squadron commander Luther Richmond. "Luther led 16 Mustangs against Vechta aerodrome outside of Berlin. He took eight ships and on the deck to do the dirty work, and the other of us got into a Lufbery over the field to draw the flak away from the Colonel's flight. The eight low ships got into a dogfight at zero altitude and shot down seven FW-190s and then went in to strafe. The Col. got direct heavy flak hit on his wing-root and went in, hitting the ground in a ball of fire. We went home and reported him KIA. Got a postcard from him three months later, a prison of war and relatively uninjured. Nothin' but filthy luck!"

dark. So when a flight is heard approaching this field that night, the boundary and floodlights are switched on. The four ships circle and peel off. Number one lands o.k. and taxies up to the control tower and parks. Noticing that the ship is German, a mechanic shoves a Very pistol into the pilot's cockpit and so captures him. He'd thought he'd been landing in France. Number 2 ship is about to set down when the floodlights are switched off. He makes the landing alright, taxies up to join his leader, and is captured, too. He then approaches the tower officer and curses him roundly for spoiling his landing (sounds like a fighter pilot, alright). No. 3 finds the lights back on, so lands, then sees that something is fishy and tries to take off again but is crashed into by an armored car. The pilot is fished out of the wreckage and hauled away. Number 4 lands and bursts into flame when the armored car turns it's machine-guns on him. That's the story, and it's true. Shows how easily one can lose himself in a fast fighter, flying where countries are small. Get confused and mistake a small peninsula for the English shoreline in bad weather, or some foolish thing like that. Only takes five minutes to cross the Straits of Dover . . .

Right at this point, Ed Heller is trying to do a pencil sketch of me. He ain't no artist, but has of late been trying to think of a hobby to pass away the long winter months. Couple of days ago he decided that whittling would be the thing. But he cut his hand and changed hobbies.

Jamboree in the Club last night. Shore had a time. Earlier in the evening went to the post movie-house and saw a USO show . . . dancing girls vintage of ought-nine; a soft-headed thumb-handed conjurer; and listened to some guy play a fiddle. So we drift over to the Club and had a couple of drinks and I grabbed a'hold of my gittar and that started the ball rolling. As the hours went along things got better and better, and when all hands were lit up to some extent we went thru the list of songs we used to know and love so well. Red River Valley and Walkin' Cane, and we are just in the middle of the Colonel's bawdy version of some Texas song when I get rambunctious and bust a couple of strings. A peachy evening. Things boomed most of the night. Some party in the hut decides he wants the lights out so he can get some sleep but his pals want to play cards. So this character grabs his .45 and boom boom boom . . . the lights go out and three holes are punched in the tin roof. Nice quiet lot of fellows in this squadron, allright.

More photos enclosed: Bob MacKean, in the hut here with our little crew. Capt. Willie O. Jackson—Operations Officer, scheduling flights and leading one hisself. Willie's a sharp customer . . . swell flyer and will take a chance. Aggressive and spoiling for a fight with anyone, any time. Bob Brown—"Bullets"—is I think our youngest pilot. Got his nickname one day when he had two 109s right square on his tail shooting all around him, and didn't know a thing about it until he wuz told of his escape after we'd returned. Jackson bounced the Jerries and shagged 'em away before they did any damage. Chet Harker in this picture looks like he's just finished facing the entire German Air Force for two solid hours.

Enuf for now. Seek to install new typewriter ribbon swindled from QM supply. Don't know what I'd have done if Mac hadn't fetched his machine over with him.

Oct. 24, '43

Was reading a wild book on RAF flying the other night, called "Wot are Yer Angels Now?" Well, angels is flying talk for altitude. Fer instance, providing the day's base altitude is zero, 20,000 feet is "Angels 20." Were the code base altitude of the day arbitrarily set at 10,000 feet, then our twenty-thousand feet would be known as Angels 10. Angels is distance above the base altitude, and distance below the base altitude is called "devils." Fer' instance, if flying at 5,000 feet in above base, you'd be flying at Devils 5.

Yesterday while plowing along with the mob up over France, the ground coordinator asks our leader, "Hallo, Curly Locks: wot are yer angels now?" and I hadda laff inside my oxygen mask becuz I'd just finished this wild story and here is the same crap being piped thru my headset. Always get a kick outta our radio chatter. Everybody has a code name (all used herein, Censor, are fictional.) But some pretty wild ones turn up. Makes for a colorful ear-full. Each pilot is assigned a code name and number. Back in the States I was at various times Saber-Red Three, Rat-Trap Fifty-three, Aqua-Marine Fifty-three, etc. Over here, however, they are much more imaginative. I would like to meet up with the characters who dream 'em up. Ground stations have code names. Pilots and squadrons and all have 'em. Everybody and anything connected with flying has a spook name. Imagine after the war three oldtime combat pilots being introduced to one another: "Hello, Red-Nose leader. Vector ninety degrees and rendezvous with two little-friends. Over to ye!" . . . "Why, Hello, Popgun 66; this is Red-Nose listening out and over to you." "Well Jeezus! If it ain't Popgun 66 from Red-Nose leader. Meet Dirty-Neck Three. Dirty Neck Three, this is Popgun 66." So that's how it'd sound. Makes confusion.

Bandits are enemy fighters. Bogeys are unidentified aircraft spotted off in the distance. Big Friends are friendly bombers. Little Friends are friendly fighters. Babies are belly-tanks. (Kitty-Kat leader, here: drop babies in one minute!)

Roger, as any fool kin plainly see, means o.k. or "understood." Also, the phonetic words are used to transmit letter of the alphabet. So if I wanted to speak my initials over the radio I'd pipe up: "Hullo, Patty-Cake control, this is Tare Peter Fox." And some of the talk turns out to be quite nice and formal. If I don't savvy a message, all I have to say is: "Hello No-Hair, this is Mohair. Say again please?" Then they transmit, "Hello Mohair, this is No-Hair: I say again, blah blah blah. Understood? Mohair, listening out." Then I acknowledge.

Common question is "Wot's the Gen?" It means wot's cookin'. Taken from the noun Intelligence, it is, and a RAF slang phrase. Intelligence is the misnomer applied to the department that gives us the latest gen on enemy tactics, defenses, etc. and briefs us upon our return.

Meet a pilot in London and ask him, "Wotcha drivin', Pal?" Meaning what type aircraft do you fly. If he mumbles "Peashooter" then he's a fighter-pilot. "T-Bolt" or "Augur-Type" means P-47. If he hollers "Vanishing American," then he pilots a particularly hot brand of medium bomber known as the B-26.

Walk into the bar and mutter "gimme glassa swill" and you get a pint of bitters. When you have it in hand and take that first sip, the proper comment is, "Bellywash!"

Having swiped some coal, now for the first time our stove is glowing red. I write a paragraph and then peel a chestnut. We split 'em two ways across the top and set 'em on top the stove. In a few minutes they're neatly done, worms and all, and we eat 'em with relish.

While on the subject of flying talk and habits, I'll tell a bit of our other language. Strictly Injun stuff, this sign lingo. Two pilots can carry on as intelligent a conversation as they'd ever accomplish clear the length of the longest bar in London—without ever having met and without speaking a word. Nods of the head and a few twists of the hand and a wiggle of the trigger finger might mean: "Howdy Neighbor. Good joint. Check that blonde in the corner!" All the while we're flying, pilots carry on silent conversations and make dirty jokes across the twenty or thirty feet of space between their respective cockpits. A jerk of the head means throttle back. A fist run forward inside the canopy means more throttle. A raised hand with fingers clawed means to change gas-tanks. A whirling forefinger followed by outstretched five-fingers means a peel-off with five-second interval between ships. Messages like that are passed from pilot to pilot clear back to tail-end Charley.

And if I looked over to Mac with a big smile and pointed downward and then made like drinking from a bottle and then gave with a series of

Lt. Col. Willie Jackson replaced Richmond as CO after Richmond was shot down and imprisoned.

pawnbroker's shrugs, he would naturally interpret as follows: "Leave us peel off and away soon as we cross the coast, land at some bomber base, and have a quicky."

Like monkeys, we talk, or injuns. Also can chat intelligently with the ship itself. Wiggle the wings and ailerons, jiggle the flipper or boot rudder. All kinds of items.

Are you getting eddicated? We got a deal on the fire for getting our Thanksgiving turkeys over here from the States. We get a flock of fat turkeys and teach 'em to fly formation. Then get an Army homing pigeon to navigate for 'em and send a couple squadrons of falcons along as escort. They land here intact and we eat 'em.

Oct. 26, '43

Weather perfect. Clean taste of Fall in the crisp wind; blue skies, trees a thousand colors. But no fly. Since the Continent was blanketed by a low and heavy overcast, thusly preventing accurate bombing, we were released till dawn tomorrow.

So Joe and Mac and me collected up a bunch of shells and shotguns and a-huntin' we did go. Before suppertime we had twenty-odd pheasants and partridges. Got into some wonderful hunting and I bet we hiked twenty miles or so. Gonna clean 'em up tonight and it's a game dinner tomorrow. It so happens that I'm the only guy who'll admit knowing how to clean these birds, but I can see where there'll be a desperate and comprehensive course in that art.

Opened up the Christmas package from home and felt that you both were parked alongside me on my bunk when I unwrapped the packages. You couldn't have shown more thoughtfulness in giving the fine book, pictures of you and of the old homestead in the album, with room for more. And a box of nuts. First time I've tasted any since I paddled out of NY harbor. Wonderful.

Archy the Gremlin has us all laughing agin. Just composed two long and involving letters to two of his Stateside gals. So he gets 'em switched and sticks 'em in the wrong envelopes. Happens to think he forgot to enclose his snapshot in one of 'em and opens it up to discover what would have been the definite and uproarious end of his romances. We naturally wish they'd gone thru the mails as wuz. What a jolt for Archy.

Flew yesterday with the squadron on a non-hostile flight, giving practice escort to a new bomber outfit. We buzzed around all over England in and out of the boxes and had a peachy time. McKibben and I finally became irritated with such non-profit proceedings and our feet were getting cold for no good reason, so by way of his radio he pleads engine trouble and peels away from the outfit at 25,000 feet. Me being his wing-man, I peel off with him and we have a hilarious good time chasing each other thru the clouds en route home. Looped and rolled and played tag thru holes and tunnels in the mountains and valleys of white cloud. Did barrel rolls around each other and made a few wicked passes at a couple of stray bombers we happened across. Get starved for a dash of that freelance flying now and then, after our bouts with that super-scientific hi-altitude formation stuff. Get down low and take off that oxygen mask, light up a smoke and raise hell for a bit.

Gotta clean up them birds. Dirty work, but sort of enjoy it. And Christmas before Halloween is unique to say the least, but still the same kind of feeling goes with it . . .

Nov. 1, '43

Heard from Craig, who is still in North Africa and wishes he were elsewhere. Rugged life and monotonous in the extreme. He sez he flew to Oran for some reason or other and had a dandy time there. About half thru with his tour of duty, which at present is forty trips across the target. And Tommy Price is down south with his '47 outfit. Norfolk, I guess. He ought to do fine, providing he doesn't get too cocky with his ship. Ain't habit-forming. Certain amount of calculated recklessness blended in with a pile of respect for this particular-type aircraft makes for a good lengthy career as a fighter pilot. Knowing one's capabilities and limitations and flying accordingly helps to prolong the fun.

Got to thinking about how odd a thing "time" is. To you earthbound mortals, time is probably a set and even-flowing something. An hour is an

Another member of C Flight, Lloyd Archibald "Rocky" Rauk (aka Archy the Gremlin) was one of Ted's early friends in the 486th. He threw up into his boot and tossed it overboard when he watched a German pilot leap from his aircraft directly into Steve Andrew's propeller. Rauk finished the war with two aerial victories.

hour and a minute is a little part of an hour. But time has sure lost its meaning for me. Have recently spent what appeared to be a half hour of fast action, involving the formulating of a half-dozen decisions, acting on same, working madly flying in quaint positions, calculating and watching instruments, and covering the sky looking out for various ships. All this at perhaps 400 mph more or less. Probably varying speeds from 100 to 500, climbing and diving vertically. I swear I could hear the seconds tick off with a gap between them, during which I could have guzzled a beer. And after the action was over I find that only fifteen or twenty seconds have elapsed. Time and distance become very distorted.

Flying and covering a mile every seven or eight seconds gives no idea of speed. A flight of a thousand miles involves no thought of miles covered, but becomes a matter of time. The first hour and a half of a flight always goes fast, seems like minutes. But then when at the turning-back point, one's hide depends upon one's ability to get the max engine performance out of his ship with minimum fuel consumption. And a hundred little tricks are put into play to save fuel. Then time slows down again. With the gas gauges moving towards the empty mark, and with a few hundred miles of cold, rough North Sea between you and England, the only thing in the world that seems at all important is gasoline. Nice stuff. Minutes stretch out into days. Seconds bloat up all out of proportion. Everything else in another world. But wot a nice restful feeling to slide over the coastline, with the knowledge that anywhere below is an airdrome where you can land and gas up before going on home. We sometimes just make the coast of England after a long fast escort mission. Peel off individually, as each pilot sees fit. I allus like to set in at a bomber base so I can heckle the bomber jockeys, who generally turn green when they see a fighter taxi up to the gas pits.

This here fog is still hanging around. Had a mission lined up for this morning, but one minute before start-engine time it was cancelled. Good thing, too, for the visibility was a half-mile and the ceiling was right on the ground.

Get a lot of fun out of takeoff. Here's a whole flock of ships parked at various spots all around the field. At start-engine time, all the propellers turn over as if they were turned on by one main control. In a moment, Thunderbolts are streaming across and around the edges of the field toward the takeoff funnel. Looks disorderly as hell, and there's some action there, too, for it adds up to a halfarse race . . . taxi forty or fifty mph, zig-zag. But each pilot knows his takeoff slot and heads for it, and we get off in amazing time. We can get 55 ships airborne and in perfect formation and heading out on-course in under four minutes, which is something of a record.

48-hour pass began at noon today, but guess I'll stick around the field again. No urge to get into town. It's nice out here in the country. May drift into the local village and see wot the pubs have to offer. Mill around and come back out to the club and have a party.

Feel another good session coming up. A harebrained lot of arguments we get into over our scotch-and-sodas. We plan grand strategy nightly, and win the war quite often.

Saw an exhibition of German flying equipment. Finest ever. Beautiful leather stuff, furs, a lot of chamois skin, and nothing very ersatz about it. Have looked over their fighters, too, and nothing sloppy about 'em.

Here's a portrait of my country home in England . . .

Nov. 4, '43

For seven days and seven nights, dense mists and strange vapors have shrouded this low country. Dense fogs have swirled about our grounded aircraft and denser fogs have enveloped our grounded pilots (courtesy of the Officer's Club, that latter). But tonight, for the first time in a long time, the stars are visible. The moon is plain to see. So we are all being good to-night and getting to bed fairly early in the hopes that there will be a mission scheduled for the morning.

You might think that we would rather not venture out on these hare-brained flights, or that we would go purely out of a sense of duty. But such is not the ease. The only hard feelings ever stirred up amongst the pilots are created when the schedule for these flying a mission is juggled, and certain pilots are replaced by others. Then the air is filled with sad cries: "Goddam it, Joe flew the last two while I sat here on my tail and now he's goin' on this 'un! And I ain't, goddam it." (And during this loudly proclaimed bitching, Joe comes swaggering by with his helmet on and buckling his chute and sneers . . . "Yaaah . . . tha Major knows who tha best pilots are in this outfit!") Plenty of bellyaching when one of the boys gets left behind (more in good weather than in foul, however) and sitting on same. Punishment for infractions of various items, such as getting caught taking off early on a two-day pass, consists of being grounded for a little while. Ten days grounded compares roughly with ninety days in the hoosegow back home.

But tomorrow I theenk we fly again, and a good one I hope. Naturally I'm slated to fly Tail-end Cholly. Last ship in the squadron and a lot of fun flying, but considerably more work, for the last ship snaps around the corners like the last guy in a crack-the-whip game on ice skates. Number one ship has it easy. He just makes a gentle turn. Then progressively back along the line, each ship had to make a steeper bank until poor Tail-end Charles has to rack his ship up on the side and really reef 'er in. And there's plenty of turning. When we get up over the bombers we're escorting, and are clocking off a neat 375 or 400, we must keep making a series of turns back and forth along the front edge of the bomber formations in order to keep back with them, for they are so slow. And clumsy.

The other afternoon Mac and I were standing behind our hut watching a bomber circle the field. It was pretty foggy so we figgered he'd land here. So we climb up on top of our hut for a better view. Around the bend he comes, wheels down, and glides in for a landing. I sez to Mac . . . he's too durn high. Mac sez to me . . . never make it this time. Now the bomber has crossed the edge of the field and is still purty high and goin' purty fast yet. I sez to Mac . . . this ought to be interesting. Mac sez to me . . . yup! By now the bomber is over the crest of the hill, which is right smack in the middle of our landing strip. Still very much airborne. We stand on top of our hut and watch the bomber float out of sight over the down slope of our field. I say to Mac . . . Shhhhh. Mac sez to me, striking a pose of intent listening with hand cupped to ear and finger to lips . . . . Shhhhh. Ten seconds drift by. Boom, rattle, rattle, boom. We look at one another triumphantly and nod our heads wisely. I say to Mac . . . we sure called that one, hey. Mac sez to me . . . pore flyin'. So we climb off the roof and go inside and play a game of casino. Then Archie come tearin' in and hollers . . . big bomber just ran thru the end of the field . . . wheeee. Knocked down a brick outhouse! Wheee!

Boy do we have fun. A lot of poker these foggy days, and am a wee bit ahead of the game at this point. Always a flurry of card-playing after payday.

Nothing much cooking tonight. Except chestnuts, which Frank Greene has displayed atop the stove. For a spell we considered sneaking out and creeping up on top of the neighboring hut in our stockinged feet. Silently like Indians, to drop a couple of shotgun shells down our neighbors' stove-pipe. But gave it up out of pure laziness.

Chapter 8

● ●

The Joy of Flying

Nov. 6, '43

Ain't nobody ever sick in this crew. Must keep the gol' danged dirty dubble-crossin' germs outta the coolin' system. I can recommend a short and delightful treatment, but I guess the pill-pusher back home would disapprove. Here's how it works. Whenever any of this bunch feels the joims a-creepin' insidiously into his fuselage and sabotagin' his corpuscles, he just lurches into the bar at our club and makes a few weak & feeble motions to the bartender. Pat (the b.t.) sets a jug of wheesky in front of the ailin' critter and sets a jug of sody-water alongside. Glub glub glub. Yeeeeeaaahoo! Zonk! Then a soak in a tubful of hot watah and into the 'ole sack. Wake up the next morning in horrible condition. Ho ho ho! Like bangin' yourself on the haid with a mallet. Feels so good when ya quit.

You say in my pictures I look older and fatter. Naturally, I have aged a couple of months in the last couple of months, but as for being fatter . . . dunno.

One day while strolling thru the narrow streets of a quaint olde English village, I spied upon a stone block in front of a Chemist's Shoppe (Walgreen's to you stay-at-homes) a scale. I hops up on the weighing platform and waits til the needle quits dancing. Then I pokes an overgrown Pennie into the slot. There wuz much sound ensuing . . . gears turning and chains revolving and levers falling into notches. The needle swung across the dial, quivered and stopped. But it wuz the 64-dollar question. The answer comes out in Stones! I never heerd of each a thing, and I stand there whoopin' and hollerin' and laughing uproariously. I scampers off down the lane and comes across a Bobby and sez hey flatfoot, wotinell is a Stone? He was very courteous and among other things, he pointed out the ancient village pump and the town hall (orating a bit of its olde history): he tells me the way to the graveyard behind 'ole Parson Meeks Church and he tells me this and that, and by the time I find out wot a Stone is I've forgotten how many Stones I weighed. Matter of fact, now I've forgotten how many Stones a pound is or how many pounds a Stone is! But me britches fit me about the same as they did when I hit this fog-stricken territory, so I guess I weight the usual 135!

Boy, do I feel good. Three days ago the mists decided to lift, and they've come and gone ever since. And whenever they've lifted long enuf for us to line up a job, we've flown, and have been doing some flying! Remember the headlines of Friday, Nov. 5th? "War's Greatest 24 Hour Air Assault Hailed." According to yesterday's paper I have before me, I went to Wilhelmshaven along with a lot of other peace-lovin' characters. 380 miles east of London! A long haul for a single-engine fighter. Plenty of excitement and a most amazing scene to behold. From my window some seven miles from the target (vertically) I could see a row of our bombers as far as the horizon queuing up for a space in which to unload their presents. And what a workout for us thin-air operators. That was on the 4th. Yesterday, the 5th, the weather was bad for combat so Joe Gerst and I get a couple of ships and load 'em up with camera film and go up to 25,000 feet and fight between ourselves. For a while. Then we tire of that, and play follow-the-leader thru great swooping dives and zooms from 500 mph down to 150. Then we seek and find some RAF bombers to make passes at, and we hound them til they shake their fists at us from the cockpit. We come down home when we get low on gas. (After a fine buzz-job on a neighboring fighter base.) That was yesterday.

Today there appears a thick cloud deck low to the ground, but things get cookin' and we sweat out a briefing (always the toughest part of any mission). We take off and immediately things start to liven up. Just get off the ground when Mac and Greene and I fly right thru the middle of a tremendous flock of birds. We each instinctively duck down in the cockpit expecting a barrage of beat-up birds to come crashing thru the windshields. But we get no victories, no damaged, and no probables from this squadron of Nazi-paid crows. Now presents itself the problem of flying our large formation up thru a solid overcast of thick milky-white cloud. We none of us are especially eager for this chore, but we gotta get thru the stuff so we tighten up our formations and plunge into the damn cloud deck. (In this case each leader of four ships goes on instruments and the three ships with him practically lock wingtips with the leader and fly formation on him, trusting implicitly to his instrument-flying abilities.)

As the clouds get thicker and the guy about twenty feet away from you fades into near invisibility, we close up tighter yet and in a couple of anxious minutes we break thru the top and into a brilliant, sunlit blue sky: As blue as blue can ever be, and now below us is flat sea of pure white clouds stretching to all horizons. Now we climb fast. (Today's flight I'm tellin' about). First the crows and then the clouds to make life interesting. We get our feet wet (leave England and head out over the North Sea). I push and pull handles and tinker around with various and sundry engine controls, trying already to save gas for the trip home. The radio begins its usual nonsense . . . whining in my ears . . . yer goin' in you're goin' in you're goin' in . . . (they're tellin' me?)

And soon our boys start a little chatter. Doesn't matter if we break radio silence this far along, for the Jerries have us all spotted long before with their radar stuff. (Interesting to know that when their radar stations pick us up, they relay the report to their fighter drones, and right now a lot of Jerry fighter pilots are running for their ships and getting their orders and making scramble takeoffs . . .) Anyway, our gang begins to look around for trouble and call in suspicious-looking specks in the sky in front of us. We at last get to our altitude and level off, on course. Spot our bombers off in the distance and meet 'em at the rendezvous point. And into our dance we go. Criss-cross top-cover for the big friends.

A beautiful day over the Continent . . . clear as a bell with the ground below plain to see, and from our height looking like a relief map. The fields and towns laid out and looking peaceful as Iowa. Trains moving along the tracks and the cities looking round and little. The sky above blue, and each of our ships leaving a round contrail, marking its exact path in a rope of newly formed cloud! A ridiculously huge mass of Flying Forts in neat geometric formations plowing along below us, very much on course and droning along in sight now of their target. We up above, in contrast to the bombers' stately procession, careening to and fro with phenomenal speed. I sit there, miles in the air with seven tons of flying machine strapped to my thin and bony tail. Me head is swiveling around like a puppy's head when he shakes a rag. The fighters range out on both sides of the bombers, looking for opposition. Then we scoot across the bombers' backs. We all kin see bandits hovering on the outskirts of our defensive circle, like a bunch of wolves slobbering in a circle around a bunch of cattle and afraid to attack because of the patrolling hunters. Ho ho! Zowie.

The target blossoms smoke for miles around and a fresh bunch of fighters comes in from England to take over our job, so over the radio comes the order for us to withdraw. So far things have been plenty tense, with guys calling in bandits from every position in the sky. We've all been flying hard and on edge for some immediate shootin, which didn't come to a focus. Now one of the boys gets into a little trouble due to the high altitude and hollers that he's gotta go down low, so he peels off from the flight and heads for thicker atmosphere. We tag along to escort for him and strike a beeline for home at a slightly non-advantageous altitude of twelve thousand feet. We slide into defensive formation and give our ships a lot of throttle to get out of the olde country as fast as possible. The ground seems close below now, and clear in every detail. Pretty soon we get over the German border in Holland, which is just as bad, being full of Jerries and their flak guns and interceptors. We slide off over the edge of the Zuider Zee and it looks like a model of same. I tilt a wing so I kin get a good look at it and find I'm right over the wee Isle of Urk.

Now that name Urk has intrigued me ever since I saw it on a map, and this is the first time I've had a chance to give it a good once over. Urk. Urk. Urk. Urk. Odd place, and I hear that the folks who live there are web-footed, live on fish-heads, and are all hermits. Cross the Zuider Zee and the strip of land and change course for home. We are still on the alert for bandits as this is no place to be at low level. Soon the long stretch of sea is crossed and England is below us, somewhere under a solid blanket of cloud. My gas is down to quarts by now, so I inform Greene that I'm leaving and will be home later in the day. So I go a-hunting for a field to land at, to refuel. Buzz along the top of the clouds looking for a hole to dive down thru, find a little, do a fancy wingover and peel down thru the stuff and come out in the middle of a balloon barrage. So it's over, under, and damn near thru balloons for a spell and then I spot a field and set down. And what do I land thru? A flock of crows. Wait till I get home. Gonna grab me a shotgun and go crow huntin' with a vengeance. So there's a typical milk run, and enuf for this windy letter.

Nov. 8, '43

Flown all the recent big deals and have sure seen some fire. The last target was one boilin' mass of smoke after the bombers finished with it. Gelsenkirchen or some such name. The good folk of the 3rd Reich are gettin' a dose of their own medicine these days. Wonder if they rue the day they laid low in the same manner Czech., Poland, Holland, Belgium, France, etc.? But no, they probably think they had the right to do the dirty work, and that nobody has the right to give it to them. An odd item, but rumor—or rather, reliable info—has it that when our aircrews parachute into target areas, say Hamburg, the citizens have clubbed and stoned them to a frazzle. But the soldiers who take the boys prisoner have protected them from the mobs, even to the point of arming them if things should get out of control.

My practical knowledge of geography improves automatically, of necessity: for if low on gas, or if busted up and scooting for home with a passel of Jerries hot on our tail, when crossing out over the enemy coast it's nice to know the shortest route from wherever we might be over to England. And too, our ground controller often radios . . . "Bandits reported in vicinity of Rotterdam," fer'instance. Must know just where in hell Rotterdam is from our present position.

So I can draw an accurate map of the coastline from Emden down thru the Terschelling Isles, Texel, Den Helder, Alkmaar, Amsterdam, Haarlem, Utrecht, Noordwijk, The Hague, Rotterdam, Dordrecht, Walcheran Island, etc. Know the Lowland terrain and same for coast of Belgium and France. You know, you and me, we've read a lot of fairy stories and novels and histories of all these countries and have many a time read of these cities and places, and when I fly over 'em all the time I find it interesting. Not much time for sightseeing, but Holland is just as you might imagine it to be: canals and ditches and swampy country; dikes and reclamation projects around the Zuider Zee. (Jerries probably flood the place if there's a land invasion). Barges and fishing boats (and flakships and torpedo boats.)

Another hoomerous item. We jerks sit around the pilots' room most of the day waiting for something to happen. English radio programs being what they are (!**@! lousy) we invariably tune in on "Calais One," a high-powered Nazi station. And they have programs that beat our hit parade. Latest U.S. hot bands, on record we presume, and a lovely-voiced gal announcer who talks our brand of English. We listen religiously to her programs and find their occasional newscast highly amusing. They introduce the newscasts with a gong: "BONG BONG BONG—We now broadcast the latest communiqués from the German Supreme Command . . . BONG BONG BONG . . . Yesterday's savage bombardment of Ruhrburg by the American barbarians resulted in the loss of ninety-three thousand, four hundred and two civilian lives, and the destruction of fourteen-thousand homes and shops. Fifteen churches and two cathedrals, complete with congregations, were utterly demolished by their indiscriminate bombing . . . BONG BONG BONG . . . Our Messerschmidt fighter aircraft destroyed ninety-nine four-engine bombers and shot the rivets outta one Thunderbolt fighter which was seen lagging behind its formation. BONG BONG BONG." (The latter was most likely one Parchesi-Joe Gerst of 486th Squadron.)

So we sit by our radio and mutter . . . Come on, Jack, finish the jabbering and give us some more jive. One day they played "Johnny Got a Zero," which probably resulted in a few hard feelings between Jerry and their allies, the Japs. We are thinking of writing in to Calais One and requesting some of our favorites. That ain't nice, tho. We sit and enjoy their radio efforts, then snap off the radio and hop into our ships and go out to bump a few of 'em off.

Other ground duties include the censoring of enlisted men's mail, which is pretty big chore. They write an awful lot of letters, and lately more and more to English lassies. The boys get around some.

More pictures of the boys . . . Capt. Andrew, a dapper gent. Shot down off New Guinea by Japs, swims five miles or so to shore, and hikes back to his field. Tom Colby, here, has holes in the head. Reads too many dime novels about flyin, but a good enuf guy when he forgets to be glamorous.

Nov. 11, '43

A fine Christmas package today from you. All say "Don't open 'til Christmas," but too late, too late. All opened by the gang here: the salve we use for our consciences is roughly this: we figger that comes an unfortunate day, we end up behind a barbed-wire fence in a Jerry PW camp. Then comes Christmas. We strain our scenery thru barbed wire and the merry lads back here open our packages with great glee, devouring the delicacies and squabbling over the non-edibles. Not so good, we say. So we enjoy what we have while we have it. Anyway, I opened my package with great relish and much thought. The soap may have been a tactful hint. I prefer to think not! The handy-dandy collapsible cribbage board meets with unanimous approval, for we've been involved in a bitter cribbage tournament for a couple of weeks now, using a pine board with holes drilled therein. And the rule book will put a definite answer to some of our more knock-down and drag-out arguments. The sewing kit has already got me sucking thumbs for needle sticks, and the maple sugar fills a spot that ain't been hit for a long time. The lads in the hut have pooled all goodies from home and it makes a chest-full of rare bits. We just finished a half dozen bottles of Sherry wine and some nuts plus crabmeat & crackers, some figs, cheese, and candied orange peel. Truly a small-scale feast of all the things we've been joking about whenever we sit down to a plate of thinly disguised Spam. Methinks the flight surgeon will have his hands full in a few hours.

And right now our portable record player, obtained by crook, is playing L'Apres Midi d'un Faun, which goes to show you how damned few records we have. A heavy rain is pounding on our tin roof and dripping upon our heads thru a number of .45-size holes. Leftenants Northrop and McKibben are playing a hot game of cribbage. Rocky is beating large hunks of coal into small hunks of coal by plunging an axe into the bottom of the coal bucket. MacKean and Joe Gerst are feigning sleep over in one corner of this madhouse. Frank Greene and Ed Heller are about to come to blows over a friendly discussion of each other's flying abilities. And here I sit on the edge of me bunk pounding away at the community typewriter.

Till tonight the weather the past three or four days has been passable enuf for us to get some flying done. We've branched out lately, and besides our very hi-altitude stuff we've been cutting loose on a brand of flying that is near and dear to our hearts. Tell you more about it later.

Enclosed find snap of pore grease-monkeys fitting belly tank to my ship. I dropped it near Wilhelmshaven somewhere on Nov. 3.

Today the weather over Europe was bad, so our group put on an airshow over the field right here for practice. What a workout. We buzzed the field in close formation, about fifty Thunderbolts, and then slid into

"Robbie [MacKean] was the nicest guy in my C Flight, and one of the original Fightin' 21st gang. He and Ed Heller left the Lake Constance area together and began strafing their way back to England. They hit some hot Jerry airdromes and Robbie got eight planes on the ground and Ed got 12 (and DSC.) But they hit Robbie's '51, and when he tried to belly in, he hit some high-lines and blew up. Killed in action."

various fancy formations and ended up with a long string of ships diving on the field in pairs and slow-rolling off the other end. A lot of fun, but just as we were coming in, a quick fog closed in and we had a helter-skelter job landing. Mechanics got a big kick out of it, anyway.

I see by the papers that the AAF in the ETO has had a deadline set. Either the Allied Air Forces knock out Germany by air power by some certain time, or then the ground forces step in and invade by land. I hope the latter never develops, for it'll be one massacre while it lasts. Our fighters and bombers can do so cockeyed much damage with such a relatively small loss of life on our side that it seems as tho it would be worthwhile prolonging the war another year or so, if it would take that much longer for air power to bring Jerry to terms. The moment our invasion barges start their engines will be the moment when American lives lost will be counted by the thousand per day, rather than the thousand per week or month. We can swing the deal by air operations solely, if they'll only give us time. When the Jerries see our thousand-ship fleets overhead they're terrified, as has been indicated by reports trickling in from the Continent. (I don't blame 'em, myself, for I'd hate to be on the receiving end of some of our raids.) And they must know that we can keep it up indefinitely and they are doomed to a slow and painful elimination, factory by factory and city by city, until nothing will be left to attack. By the type of flying we've been introduced to of late, I think that things are definitely coming to a focus now. New weapons will be introduced by us and air power can finish things if only the ground generals can swallow their pride and pigeonhole their ancient and obsolete traditions. Jerry morale is on the skids and it ain't improving as our siege progresses.

Mac and I have from noon tomorrow until noon Saturday off. We hope that rains linger until we get back. We hate to miss out on any fireworks.

Chapter 9

....

Thunderbolts

Nov. 15, '43

Weather been closed in for two days now, and the last job we pulled was an escort job taking bombers in to their target, which was Munster. Had a lot of fun on that deal. One of the Forts develops flak trouble near the target and peels away from his formation, heading for home alone. Now Jerry likes to see a lone bomber. Easy meat, and usually a couple '190s will attack and knock him down. Anyway, I spot this straggler and call him in to Frank Greene who is leading our four ships, so we peel off away from the squadron and cover this cripple on his way home. Frank and Leo and Mac and me, and we have much sport escorting this guy. We circle over him and head into various unidentified aircraft who start for him, and then when England is in sight we roll around him and zoom and play like porpoises for a while. It turns out that the crew of this Fort is so happy to've had our company that he puts in a good word for us when he gets home, and the next day our flight is commended in orders for an "excellent escort" job. (When really we just goofed off and had a little innocent fun).

My ol' pal Cutler is leaving the outfit tomorrow, having been transferred to the Ferry Command as the aftermath of a small-scale knockdown-drag-out brawl a while back. Too durned bad and a very dirty deal, both for him and for us, as Frank is one of the hottest pilots in the group. Perfect temperament for fightin' and flyin'. Sorry to see him leave, but he'll be back before long, if I know Frank.

95

Yesterday got a brand new ship; she's the new Thunderbolt with the so-called secret engine that develops 2,000-plus HP when needed. Which makes me the proud possessor of the fastest ship anywhere. Should walk away from or catch anything that flies these days. And she's mine all mine. The boys are workin' on her down in the hangar, and after the acceptance check is finished and after I put a dozen hours on her to break in the engine, I'll be able to cut loose. First saw her this a.m. when my crew chief, German, was running the engine up. Rocky and Joe were standing by watching, and she sounds throaty and plenty powerful. When German spots us he gives us a big grin and a wave. So today I arrange to have some of the boys taken off KP and put on a special detail, which consists of them sanding the rough camouflage paint down to a smooth, fast surface. Dunno why those fatheads back in the States keep sending us ships with a built-in headwind. Also this slave-labor comes in handy, but the boys would a lot rather be out on the line working on an airplane than washing pots and kettles in the mess hall.

Franklyn Greene led the 486th Fighter Squadron's C Flight. His P-47 was named *Snow White,* and he requested that the seven other pilots in the flight name their aircraft after the various dwarves (a notion that Ted boycotted). He scored three aerial victories.

The other day flying on the lastest combat mission, I hears over the RT a hot call from some bird that ten-plus bandits are looming up off our rear quarter, so I flick on my gun switch. Inasmuch as the bandits turn out to be another '47 outfit, the encounter falls thru, and I forget to turn my guns off. A little later I make a hasty emergency maneuver to avoid a head-on collision with a flight of four '47s from some other outfit, and while snatching controls I haul back on the stick real fast and inadvertently squeeze the trigger.

Now right at this stage of the game I'm taking a quick scan of my engine instruments while twisting my head from the sky on the right to the sky on the left. And out of the corner of my eye and striking my absent mind a terrific blow, I see a flash of fire and a cloud of smoke and simultaneously feel the ship give a shake and a shudder. First thought: Pore Ted's had it!—figuring automatically that some Jerry has snuck up behind and wuz givin' me both barrels. Second thought: Keerist! Me engine done blew up! Third thought: Uh-huh. Knew it alla time. Left the gun-switch on! All of which took place in one second and taught me another lesson. Learn something about this racket every day.

The new cribbage board has been doing double duty ever since it hit the ETO. I got whupped today by Gignac by about forty pegs.

Will write again pretty soon when something happens worth writing about. Letters will furnish copy for my tall stories when I git back home!

Nov. 18, '43

Non-eventful day. Matter of fact, the past couple have been slow. They have the lousiest weather over here. The sky changes from hour to hour . . . one hour blue, then a bit later on there'll be a half dozen different kinds of clouds floating merrily around. Spent the day puttering about my new aircraft. Painted the white stars on the fusilage and wings, touched up chipped places with a spray gun. Sandpapered her nose. How'd you like that treatment? And joked around with grease monkeys. Squadron flew a practice mission today but I stayed on the ground on account of becuz this fog here seeped into my chassis and gave my one good corpuscle the sniffles. Been hiding from the Doc so as not to be grounded, as my cold ain't bad enuf to keep me from flying combat, but I didn't want to risk my eardrums on a practice flight. So on the ground I stood with a bottle of beer clutched in one grimy paw and watched the air show. The boys pulled a practice strafing attack on the field and they really worked it over for a while, beating up and down about five feet off the ground. Looked fine and sounded better.

Small poker party in the hut last night. Played til the wee hours. Won twenty pounds, which tends to make me well again. Every now and then we'd dispatch some gent over to the Club to have a couple of canteens filled once again with wine. Nice little evening and a nice big head. Also took in movie called "Spitfire." Goes by that name in the States, but here is titled "So Few for So Many" and is the story of the Spitfire fighter ship and the guy who designed it. Swiped the aerodynamics from the seagulls, which flop about this ol' island. Fine show and realistic flying shots, realistic enuf to make us cringe now and then.

We just have a tiny stove in our hut, two feet high and eight inches in diameter, burning coal, wood, shotgun shells, coke, high-octane gas, etc. Wasn't throwing enuf heat, so tonight Rocky and I remove the firebrick lining with the aid of an axe, and the cockeyed thing is cherry-red from the floor clear up the stove-pipe and no one can get within six feet of it. We fix 'em, allright.

The Forts have doing a job on various points in Norway the past few days. We can't go along for it's too blamed far for us. One day we'll have auxiliary tanks maybe that'll get us that far and back. Now we could get that far, but not back. Which would be un-humorous. I wouldn't doubt but what the targets are important. Heavy-water installations, research labs, etc. Who kin tell?

We flew at night a while back, just taking off, circling the field, and shooting a couple of landings. To get the horrible feel of black-out landings again. Not a ground light visible from the air in this country at night. Landing is about like driving a Rolls-Royce automobile off the lip of the Grand Canyon and waiting for the sonuvabitch to hit the bottom.

Nov. 21, '43

Flown only once since last letter. Weather increasingly foul in these parts. Escorted a bunch of B-17s into the Ruhr Valley. No opposition whatsoever outside of a lot of inaccurate flak. So that one turned out to be another milk-run affair.

Last night, Saturday, most of our three squadrons went over to a party that a B-17 Bomber Group threw for us. The gang of us load into a couple of Army trucks and away into the fog we go. This Fortress base is only some 15 miles from here, but we took a cool two hours getting there, on account of becuz we got lost any number of times. We crossed one cock-eyed railroad track four times at the same place that I know of but finally ended up at the right bomber field. If we get so lost in the fog in a lousy truck, figure out how lost we get driving a Thunderbolt thru these mists!

We are greeted at this bomb outfit by the pilots, co-pilots, navigators, and bombardiers of this bombardment group that we have escorted a half-dozen times, and they really throw a party for us: rum, scotch, and beer flow freely in all directions until early in the morning, and at that stage of the game I see two Chaplains layin' criss-cross in a puddle on the floor, heads pillowed in brass spittoons. But all pilots are more or less vertical and with fresh drinks continually tilted skyward. Helluva party. Those bomber boys lead a tougher life than do we. Heard many a wild tale of some of their combats with Jerry fighters. This is the gang that brought back a jackass from Africa on one of their shuttle-raids from here to there and back again—bombing hell out of Germany going and coming. Also the same outfit that has three flying officers named Ready, Willing, and Able!

Today, Sunday, we wake up early and take a gander at the weather. Cold swirling fog again, so I hop back into the sack and snooze til noon for a change. Had what was technically called a steak for dinner, with chocolate ice cream for dessert. This ice cream is made from powdered milk and other ersatz goodies, and tastes like it. This afternoon Mac and I play cribbage for a while then play a hot game of rummy til suppertime. Then a little stud poker, and not a very exciting day. But no fun outside, chilly and wet, and as most of us have colds we're doctoring them up with our own prescriptions. Feel better all the time. Good medicine. One four-finger snifter every ten minutes for three days and something's bound to happen.

Haven't been off the field for six weeks or so. But have five-day leave coming up the 5th of Dec. Mac and I will probably spend it all in London, touring about, seeing the tourist-type sights (you bet), taking in the shows. Would go to Scotland but can't face the train service. Absolutely bad.

My new ship is about ready to take to the air. Looks fast and I'm eager to get the slow-time done so I can open 'er up.

See this little clipping about fast group take-offs (55 ships airborne and in formation in three minutes.) Well, Col. Mason is our Group commander and it's about our outfit. Hot rocks, we keep telling ourselves. I'll also vouch for the uphill runways. Adds a catapult effect to our takeoffs.

Had letters from Tommy and Len lately, full of flying chatter. Tom's doing o.k. and Len seems to be resigned to flying those B-24s over there. A lot of the B-24s over here and I may be seeing Len on this side of the Atlantic before long. That would be fine, but I'll take no responsibility on the first party we throw.

Nov. 25, '43
This wuz Turkey Day. The hunk I had for dinner wuz corn fed and muttered "OINK" under its breath when it wuz alive.

Back early this a.m. from 48 hours leave pleasantly, I think, spent in Cambridge. Mac and I hit town about suppertime and hopped an autobus . . . one of those top-heavy double-decker models, complete with coal-burning auxiliary fuel system trundling along behind. A racy design, that. Anyway we ride this groaning machine uptown and bail out at the market square. This square is some layout. A big cobblestoned quadrangle in the heart of town, thronged with people shopping around at the various open-air shops. Vegetable stands and souvenir shacks and farmer's carts loaded down with cabbages and turnips and a few crates of chickens. And on the streets surrounding the market are a varied bunch of characters indeed! A couple of hundred guys and gals going every which-way on their bicycles . . . old gents with chin whiskers and your squirts from the many local universities (with their flowing black capes streaming off their shoulders . . .) Ol' gals and young pretty gals all pedaling as if their lives depended upon their getting somewhere in a matter of seconds. A lot of American soldiers, mostly airmen, standing on the sidewalks and leaning against the buildings, all gazing idly about and waiting for the pubs to open up. A lot of dames in uniforms, too. WAAFs and ATS gals and a few WRNS. Now and then a couple of U.S. WAACs stroll by. Mac and I see four of 'em that look like they've been swinging a sledge-hammer for a living. Their combined weight must have exceeded a good eight-hundred or a thousand pounds. Think of it. A half-ton of good ol' American female!

Anyway, in this town you gotta know somebody in order to get a night's lodging and meals, so we drive on up to the English-Speaking Union, which is a slick outfit operating in that city. They fix us up with a room in a private home and phone up a good restaurant and make reservations for us for dinner that night. The gracious lady at the desk tells us what's cooking in town that night: at the theatre, movies, and tells us where there's a dance. So we have dinner at a fancy place called Tony's (or Toni's, rather!) There we pick the tendons off a couple of teeny chicken legs and wash down a mess of brussels sprouts and turnips with a gulp of red wine, and light up a Lucky. By now the bars and pubs have opened, so we leave this Greasy Spoon and lurch out into a full-fledged blackout. (Go into the closet, shut the door and chink the cracks with rags. Then shut off the light and you'll see nothing at all. Like us.) Feature a whole city blacker than that after dark, and you'll see what we're up against at night in these parts. If the moon ain't out, you're sunk. At first we slink along, feeling our way, putting one foot slowly ahead of the other and wiggling it around as a feeler. After a block of this slow progress, we strike out manfully, missing turns, tripping over curbs, and richocheting off the spooks traveling the other way. Then down a narrow crooked alley and branch off into another narrower, crookeder alley and fumble for third doorknob on the left.

Into a blaze of light and smoke and a gang of pilots and airmen and uniformed gals and a few civilians. This is a popular jernt called the Purple Cow or Royal Bull or some such outlandish name as that. Four sly barmaids behind the bar, pumping out pint after pint of ale and beer. Mac and I case the joint and guzzle a couple of pints of the stuff and shoot the breeze with a couple of sergeants from the RAF who tell us they are on a survival-leave. The night before they'd parachuted from a crippled bomber over England, leaving the dead to ride the ship down, upon its return from a night raid on Berlin. So being granted a generous day off, they are out celebrating the fact that they are out celebrating.

We get tired of this place and lurch out into the night again and hit a few more bars and then take in the big dance hall. A lot of U.S. uniforms there and a bunch of skirts. Mac whirls one around the dance floor for a while; I'm having a beer and stringing the barmaid along with a pack of lies. Thus goes the evening, and we end up trying to find our rooming-house in the dark.

We teeter down Jesus Lane (the right street) and stumble into: (1) a churchyard, where I bruise my shins severely on an ancient tombstone and dispatch the ghosts with a round of angry profanity, (2) a bobby, who shines his torch into our eyes, thus utterly blinding us for a good ten minutes, (3) an iron picket fence, where I rip Joe's best trench coat that I'd borrowed for the trip. Finally, by much match-striking we roughly locate ourselves. The address we seek is 51. I find 55 and Mac finds 48. I find 52 and Mac finds 50, so we beat on the door and go in and go to bed at 51 Jesus Lane. Helluva spot for a couple of sinners.

The next morning we shop around and bust into an antique shop. Old swords and casques and wicked knives and old keys and cobwebs, and the whole joint is so cluttered up with junk you can't take two steps in any direction. The old gent who operates it asks us what we're looking for. We say we are just pottering around and he sighs and sez there's too bloody much of that kind of thing going on . . . not at all like the old days, when ardent collectors of guns and relics came in looking for one particular thing. He sez that after Dunkirk he sold out his complete collection of cutting knives and stabbing knives, durn it. Then he grabs up an old rag and begins to dust off various worthless items and informs us that we ain't exactly welcome if we don't know what we want. So away we go, thrown out of an antique shop!

The rest of the day is spent in like manner, and we spend the evening making the rounds of the pubs and bars, and catch a late train out of town. What a trip home.

First off, the rattler is an hour late. Then we sleep past our station and at four a.m. find ourselves standing on a black and frigid crossroads in a wee little town. We are alone. Starts to drizzle. No cigarettes. Dunno where we are. Cold and windy. A couple of hours later, a gay little truck wheezes to a stop and a chubby, cheerful postman invites us to make the rounds with him of the local territory. It will take us near to the field, so in we hop and away we go.

This little truck is mighty old and rolls over the country roads like a washtub washing out to sea. The gent driving hums and sings English ditties and stops now and then to throw out a mail bag. He drives with abandon and speed, and tears thru the night with practically no headlights . . . and makes all the countless twists and turns of the road with great skill. He honks his horn now and then just to hear it peep, and every time he honks it he laughs with gusto and hollers at Mac and me . . . "'Ere!! Eyen't tha' a dandy 'orn naiow, you blokes!!!" We thunder thru a forest and a rabbit runs out in front of the car and our driver swings the wheel violently and runs it down . . . then he throws on all the brakes, and leaps out and picks the rabbit up and tosses it behind the seat and sez, "First one I got in near to a year! Cor!! Th' missus'l make a stew naiow, an if it's too broke up to make stew out of, I'll feed it to the bloody cat!!!" And off we go.

We get out in a town near to here and phone up for a jeep and ride into camp just in time for breakfast. Wot a night. Met more cockeyed characters.

My cold is gone. The Cambridge cure. Worked on my new ship today and got a letter from Tom Price this p.m. Sez profanely that he quit his old Holyoke gal after he found out I'd gone with her. Laughed so hard I liked to've croaked! Tom's getting a lot of '47 flying done and oughta be over here soon. Still a poker sharp and claims to've cleaned up 500 bucks last month. He'll get along. Enclosed is clipping on Bremen raid we escorted. Berlin at present seems to be the target for our mass attacks. Wouldn't care to be living there now. I think that after rationing in the States is over I'm going on a diet. Nuthin' but rare steaks. I will buy up all the Spam on the market and put it on the train tracks and observe its destruction. I will corner the turnip and brussels sprouts market and bury it all under quicklime, too.

How're things back home this winter? Any trouble getting fuel oil? Don't worry. Houses over here are uniformly damp and cold inside. I've gone into three different rooms of a big home here and seen three distinct types of cloud formations hanging below the ceilings. I don't see why they build houses at all. They could just set tables and chairs out on a vacant lot somewhere and settle down. It's much nicer outside.

The squadron is still going along with a perfect record. The climate keeps us waging a constant battle against head colds, which are hi-altitude pilots' worst enemy. We eat aspirins and ammonium chloride tablets (for coughing at hi-altitude, which can lead to filling one's oxygen mask with all sorts of interesting items). We sniff our benzedrine inhalers so much that my nose is becoming deformed. We spray our noses and throats before each flight. We hook down a jigger of scotch nightly. We sleep thru breakfasts and play poker til three in the morning. We have a lot of fun. It's a great life and full of interest every minute.

C-Flight of the 486th Squadron (tha's us) finally got around to putting Snow White and the Seven Dwarves on its ships. Frankie Greene leads the eight-ship flight, so he got stuck with a wishy-washy picture of Snow White painted up on the side of his ship's cowling. Rocky got Dopey's picture painted on his ship (fits him to a T). Northrop got grumpy (perfect!) Mine isn't painted yet, but guess I'll get Happy or Sneezy or something. It ain't my idea of what oughta be painted on a fighter ship, but I s'pose I'll have to string along with the boys.

Enuf for tonight, ain't it?

Nov. 29, '43

Glad you liked the sketch of C-Flight's Nissen Hut. We got "Psychopathic Ward" chalked on the door so people will know where we live. Tonight Rocky picks up a shotgun and sends a wad of shot thru the back door, from within, to see how powerful these Limey shotgun shells are. Powerful enuf to blow a hole in our door, we find.

Enclosed find clipping from *Stars & Stripes* concerning last Friday's raid on Bremen. Brother was that a cold flight . . . In our cockpits we have a long, flexible hot-air tube that the pilot can direct around the greenhouse as needed to melt frost away. I flew the whole mission with the hose stuck first down one boot and then down the other. Felt dandy. It was a cold flight with respect to the temperature, but otherwise it was plenty hot. Our outfit knocked down three Jerries dead and two others as probables. Sadly enuf and inasmuch as I was being flung off the turns and laboring upside down and backwards to keep track of Mac, I didn't get a shot at any of these '109-driving jerks. Me trigger finger has a horrible itch these days.

Had a lot of fun today on a similar raid. Flew as a spare ship behind the squadron, and when one of the boys aborted (was forced to pull away from the outfit and return home) Ed Heller, also flying spare, and I both make a mighty effort to fill in the gap. We reach the opening at the same time and neither of us will give in to the other and go on home. So where there should have been a four-ship flight, we have a five-ship mess. I edge in between a couple of ships and cut some guy out and tack onto the leader (Gignac). Pappy is highly upset at seeing his neat flight turned into a shambles, and he jumps up and down in his cockpit, taking his whole ship up and down with him, and therefore taking five ships up and down in an amusing maneuver. He shakes his fist at me and motions: get the hell outta there, Faro! But I signal him back in an unmistakable gesture of refusal. Now Ed also cuts in and stays, so finally one of the rightful members of the flight has to bust away (a new replacement pilot, who is quite bewildered) and the four of us go merrily into the Continent.

We drive in pretty deep and meet our bombers and commence our top-cover escort work. Eight of us drift away from the others and prowl around the sky to the front of the bombers, looking for trouble. We scare off some bandits at various times but never get a chance for an attack. We were primed to the gills for action today and I wuz disappointed not to cut loose at something. We lost none of our bombers, however, so our mission was completely successful, according the 8th Fighter Command, which sez that we fulfill our duty when we accomplish our main objective, which is to protect the bombers. But we are always a bit irritated when Jerry doesn't try to interfere with 'em.

My new ship (known lately as the "Hangar Queen") is about ready now. She looks slick and I'm eager to try 'er out.

Ran into some pretty clouds today. Rather on the bleak side, though . . . looked like a field of plowed-up snow. Wear a lot of duds flying now: two suits of woolen long-johns, wool shirt and pants and a heavy sweater. Wool and silk sox in about four layers, sheepskin boots and leather jacket, which tend to keep me comfortable at altitude.

How about that 20-day leave of Len's! Holy smoke. They must be gettin' soft-hearted back in the States. Only leave I've had since Pearl Harbor is the week off I got when I was at Luke Field in Arizona. And I had to bust my wrist and concuss my haid to get that. Ho ho ho. Have five days coming up in December, tho. Ha ha! Sorry that Len dislikes his present brand of flying, but he doesn't have much to say about where he goes and does from now on. I'm lucky to be where I am doing what I am. Just my speed, and I do mean speed.

So one of my letters was chopped to bits by the censors. Too bad. Must have slipped a bit in my enthusiasm over this racket.

Dec. 4, '43
Any glaring errors in my typing may be laid directly at the door of the whole gang of pilots . . . for tonight we threw a party which wuz a party. For dinner we had roast partridge with dressing and all the fixin's. Wot a feed (courtesy of skeet-guns and local wildlife) After dinner we made whoopee with a bunch of local frails which wuz invited in by various operators. Plenty to eat and drink, etc.

The group flew again today and came home with three more victories. Which makes the score nine to five, in favor of our outfit. One of the lads had an exceptionally spectacular shot. He chases this Hun down from twenty-thousand feet clear to the deck, a whoopin' and hollerin' in his mike all the way down. He finally nails this bird cold at about six thousand feet and pulls up to watch the crash. The Jerry augers into a Belgian farmhouse at about six-hundred mph and explodes nicely, which was fine for our boy, rough on the Jerry, and c'est la guerre for the farmer. Having flown about every mission in November, thereby getting ahead of the rest of the lads, I had to sit this job out on the dirty ol' ground and listen to proceedings on the VHF radio.

If I'm not scheduled for a possible morning flight, I'll take off early for London. Leave from the 6th to the 10th, and there'll be hell to pay. Warm rooms and beautiful dames floating about. Radiators and hot water.

Our wee bit of a stove is insufficient for this weather. If you sit three feet from it you're cold. We sit around playing poker in the evenings dressed like Eskimos in fur boots and jackets. Getting out of bed early in the mornings is what hurts, tho. By then, of course, the fire is dead and the inside temperature is down around freezing or thereabouts. The only thing that makes us hop out with any show of spirit is the thought that we might have fresh eggs for breakfast. Twice a week, as a treat, and as pilots only get 'em there's damn near a mutiny from other quarters.

Flew my new ship today for the first time. Some crate. A few bugs in 'er yet but she handles mighty sweet. Went up to 35,000 feet over the field and ran a few engine tests. Nice baby. Just wore a sweater and no boots and I liked to've got an over-all frostbite. Bet it wuz sixty below zero up there. It wuz pretty clear and I could see a good hunk of England laid out below me like a relief map. Went thru some clouds that were so dandy that I felt like getting out and hopping around on 'em. They were just the right type of clouds that it looked like a guy'd sink about knee deep in 'em, like he would in a snowbank. And when I came down from altitude this morning, I rolled and looped and did slow and easy wingovers and flew upside down to my heart's content. It's nice to fly alone for a change. Not having to look out for fifty other ships flying formation.

Come to think of it, I honestly think that you folks at home need more morale-building than we do over here. If our gang, meaning Archy and Joe and Ed and Mac and Leo and me, is any representative group, we are sure enuf self-sustaining. Our life is absorbing and exciting and we're doing just about what we want to be doing, with no distracting flag-waving odds and ends to get in our way. We fly against Jerry and he flies against us. He tries to outfox us and we outfox him, generally. So our job is simple, I think, compared with yours. You gotta try to live a normal, conservative life every day. If you see what I'm driving at. Mebbe you are enjoying yourself at home, say. Then you think . . . Keerist, 3,000 miles away is pore ol' Unka Ted, living a life of hardships and trials. Nuts. I'm well fed, with my own kind of people and happy like the skylark, doing what is to me a rather enjoyable job of flying. Like getting paid for poaching in the Paul Bunyan Forest Preserve. So don't any of you birds get the idea that I'm having a rough time of it, for I'm not.

Will write a postal card from London, if I can. And I think I can . . .

Dec. 4, '43 (same day)
(One-half page ripped out by Censor) . . . We'd flown the day or so before and knocked down three '109s. So this day we are feeling pretty hot. The weather is not good. Sort of a haze on the ground and went to briefing feeling cocky. The CO, Joe Mason, gives us the dope on the coming flight. We have the map in front of us showing the routes of the various fighter groups and the routes of the bomber Task Force. Colonel Joe sez Let's go boys, and we scamper off to our ships and sit there waiting for the zero hour. So off we go, and what a sky! We set course and slide close together for an instrument climb thru the lowest clouds. I bust up thru the lowest deck of cloud and into the most fascinating hunk of scenery I've ever seen. Broken golden chunks of pure beauty scattered recklessly below. Absolutely unforgiveable to throw such a sight away on them what can't see it. Above and around me were fairylike castles of wispy vapors, like a scene from some outlandish story book. On the way upstairs I thought it just wasn't true. No one but a very few privileged characters in this world should be allowed a look at this sight! Then I think . . . look at those little bitty wings willya! (they only stick out about fifteen feet on each side) . . . just what the hell keeps me up here . . . I look over the nose of my ship and see the silver disk of the prop and see the gremlins dancing over my cowling, too. It's not possible for most people to see such stuff. Clouds loom up before me and break around me and I finally break thru the top of all the different cloud decks. And now below are all of 'em: three lovely, absolutely sherry-wine sorts of cloud decks below. Above is nothing but brilliant blue sky and a blinding sun. And around me are forty or fifty other

Thunderbolts, all in perfect formation and climbing at an angle to the horizontal of what looks to be about thirty degrees. And as I check all this, I know it's just momentary but at the same time wish sort of hopelessly that I could freeze it and make it last a year. But now is the time and no other, and tomorrow it'll be gone and just a memory. And then I think ahah! Wot a mellerdrammer! All this scheme of the sky with the squadron climbing up through, as though in an air review. And ahead lies what? Hmmm? Were it a B-picture out of Hollywood, the trailer would announce: Hun pilots in swastika-marked rocket-ships, thirsting for our hide, or blood, or whatever.

So up we climb, over the clouds, over England, over the North Sea and on into the thin cold air over Occupied France and Belgium. Now, in its bored tone, our radar station reports many bandits over the Dutch Islands. (Flushing, Walcheren, and the third named quite appropriately: Over-Flakee.) So we become individually alert as all hell, drop belly tanks, and drone on toward the rendezvous with the bombers. We make rendezvous, shag around with a flock of Jerries, break escort, and then we go on home. Four of us of C-flight take a straggler B-24 back to England. We get paid after we hit home base, on the ground o.k., and some of us figger we earned this month's. It was payday for three of the other boys shortly before.

So today I fly again. Another one, and the most spectacular penetration to date. Used the other day's experiences to the best advantage, playing it cagey on route in to meet our bombers. Briefing as usual with a few additional admonitions. Into our duds and a jeep to the flight line and into our ships. Zero hour and off again. We set course, climbing to altitude, always boring our way toward the rendezvous point. Bombers' target today is deep in the Ruhr Valley, (Happy Valley again) and we meet them just as they leave their target. So there they appear out of the flak, hundreds of 'em, in beautiful formation. Those bomber boys have plenty of guts, and it takes plenty of guts to fly like they do . . . precise, geometric formations, boxes line-astern, with the formation designed to give maximum firepower against attacking fighters. And our big friends are perfect targets for the countless flak guns that lie along their path.

So today the ground is plain to see below. Rivers shine in the sun and canals and lakes are silver strips and patches. A few scattered low clouds slide along below, and our bombers are high enough, up around 25,000 feet, to be laying long strips of grey contrails. So our outfit breaks up and Thunderbolts in fours and eights zigzag to and fro over the big boys. Thunderbolts cruise above and below and range out to the side of this show, with everybody and his brother laying contrails, and the sky is cut up with a most fantastic pattern of these long and ropey cloud tracks. Here and there I see lone bombers sliding out of formation, diving for the low clouds and heading for home with ten men in each. One section—eight ships of our bunch—spots a bunch of Jerries queuing up on a few stragglers and goes down on an attack: with a net result of no bombers lost, no fighters lost, and three Jerries blown up. When our relief comes in to take over escort, we head for home, more or less individually. Four of us band together and I run across Mac, so we fly home low over the countryside, sweating out our gas, dodging a couple of volleys of flak, and finally we hit the Channel and then it's England. We barrel-roll our way home and the day's flying is ended.

So there in a nutshell is a shot of our last couple of trips. Happy birthday, Mom, and have sent along an Air Medal, which most of us found in our mailboxes the other day. Wait a while before blowing about Uncle Ted and His Speedy Aircraft, for the citation reads something about meritorious achievement in the eating of Spam and sprouts thrice per day for many moons.

Foggy again now, so nothing cooking. But an amusing incident. Our communications officer, Chop-Chop Meyers, knows his radio but his fingers are strictly thumbs. He gets ahold of a jeep today and having never driven a car before, he backs it thru the CO's Nissen hut, pushing in the front and leaving just a roof of corrugated tin. Pore Chop-Chop.

Dec. 10, '43
Back last night from five-day leave spent most aimlessly in London town. Mac and me, and a swell time doing nothing. Hauled in at four a.m. and had a fine time reading our mail and waking the rest of the boys up.

Had a big fog around here a while back, plenty thick stuff . . . couldn't see but about five feet. Now this dark night, one of the local ground officers starts driving into town in his jeep. He creeps down the winding road and suddenly finds himself surrounded by steep hills no matter which way he turns. Hills to the rear, in front, and on both sides. After driving in wee circles for a while he dismounts and investigates the situation afoot. And soon finds out that he and his jeep are at the bottom of a great big bomb crater. The truth, s'help me.

Don't try holding your breath till I get a leave in the States. Might be three months, six months, or two years. No idea. Might even ship out direct to India or some equally odd neighborhood. Dunno. Have now logged thirty sorties over the old country, and after fifty or so more may be able to predict this leave stuff with some degree of accuracy. At any rate, the AAF still puts us where they want to put us, and when, and we don't have too much to say about it. We're glad we're in this neck of the woods instead of being stuck down in the Pacific somewhere. In our cold climate we don't have to mess around with tropical bugs and quinine and stuff like that there; and too, over here most of the codes of combat are followed, more or less . . . i.e., no shooting folks outta their parachutes, more or less fair treatment of captives, etc. And off duty we live like white men. But the ETO has the general reputation, verified by pilots who've flown both theaters, of being the Big League of all aerial combat circles. The Hun is sly and skilled and flies some of the best aircraft in the world. Both sides over here lay elaborate ambushes for each other and many times it comes down to plain and fancy outfoxing the other guy. Fighter tactics on both sides are quite similar—one, however, being offensive and the other defensive. Our being defensive, oddly enough, most of the time when escorting bombers. So it's a case of leadership and individual flying ability when the two forces tangle it up. And as proven by our victories and losses, we outclass Jerry seven ways from Sunday when it comes to that.

Yes, my guardian angel beats the one I sent home in the picture by a million miles. Wot a queen! She poked her head into the cockpit twice last Sunday within ten minutes. First time she sez woops, take 'er easy, Bud! Second time she smiled sweetly and sez there's the field, honey. I sed stick around baby, but I wuz so busy shooting a red-hot landing that by the time I got well on the ground and looked around for her, she'd pulled a fade on me.

This deal whereby I meets the queen is roughly this: flew to Paris with the boys to bring the Forts home that afternoon, and when we get near home it's very plain to see that some ugly weather has closed in around our field. Diving down from altitude I kin see a lot of sunlit ground below me, and up in front toward home there is a wall of low clouds and fog and haze. Zonk, we plunk into the stuff and immediately each pilot begins to concentrate and sweat cockleburrs. The group breaks up and the squadrons break up and now the air is full of flights of fours and pairs and various single ships all milling around at astounding speeds and trying to locate the field. The ground is invisible from five hundred feet, and everybody is half on instruments and half contact, which is not a habit-forming way to fly a fighter at all. I kin tell once when I am near the field, for four Thunderbolts loom up at me in a peel-up for their landing, and to avoid meeting one of 'em I break away sharply. The four of us that are still together have a few more close ones like that, and decide amongst ourselves to go away and land somewhere and come in later on when the traffic situation is better. We're getting low on gas, too. Leo hollers that he "gotta land, I only got fifteen minutes gas left." So away we buzz, flying low and looking for a field.

Leo spots one and drops his gear and I follow close behind him, and he sets down o.k.—landing very long but o.k.—and I hit the runway a half mile behind him. So he now comments thru his radio that there is a helluva big ditch in the middle of the runway. So I clamp my brakes on and hit this ditch a little crooked and start sliding sideways down the runway doing about ninety per. This is where the guardian angel shows up the first time and mutters at me. I get straightened out somehow with prop-blast and rudder and taxi up behind Leo. And we find that we've landed at a new field with no gas facilities. Still under construction. When I landed I noticed Limey workmen scattering right and left. Ho ho. Leo sez he ain't got enuf gas to take off and fly home, so pretty soon I radio home and ask 'em to clear the field for me. They think I am still in the air and I don't tell them different, becuz I am going on leave this afternoon and can't see sitting on a foreign airbase sucking my thumb. So off I go into the soup, full power and flaps and I hop over the ditch and lose contact with the ground right away. For the soup has thickened considerably. I let down to a hundred feet. I miss a hilltop by an inch, so I climb on instruments up thru the top where it's nice and sunny. But me gas is low and so I can't stay up in the sunshine all day, so down to a hundred feet again, and I just happen to catch a glimpse of my field. Knowing I'd never find it in the fog again, I pop my wheels down and come in downwind, hotter'n a two-buck pistol. Hit the ground two-thirds of the way down the field and durn near nose over three or four times trying to get her stopped. As I turn around, I notice I am off the field and in a wheat stubble-field near a creek bottom some distance from camp, so I taxi back to the line, and I pass a fire truck and a meat-wagon and a few jeeps that are tearing off across the field, and I wonder what's cooking. It turns out they had observed the first part of my hare-brained landing, and when I'd disappeared over the hill going like a scared jackrabbit they'd figgered that they had some business for sure. Some fun, this English weather. (Leo didn't get home til the next day). That evening I took off for London with Mac, feeling fine and dandy. We came back a day early for some reason and went flying. Flew around shooting at each other with camera-guns.

Enuf of this letter, as there are three or four characters hanging around me like vultures waiting to use the machine . . . bye-bye.

Dec. 17, '43
No combat for ten days or so. I got pretty far ahead of some of the boys due to their being sick, lame, or lazy, so of late I've been forced to sit around while they've gone out. No justice. But am slated for the next haul,

"So there I was . . ." A post-mission debriefing. Third from the right is Mac, Ted's best pal and flight mate.

which was to've been today. We awoke to find the field shrouded in fog and didn't expect to have to fly. But along about noon an order comes thru that we're due over Germany shortly, so we go to briefing and sit and shudder and listen to various bad-weather flying techniques being bandied about. We put our chutes in our ships and sit around the pilots' room sweating out the zero hour. Outside the weather is absolutely lousy, and folks feel grim at the thought of having to take off and climb forty or fifty ships up thru twenty-thousand feet of that stuff in close formation. At the last minute the show is cancelled, and everybody cuts loose with a whoop and holler of pure relief. A last-minute pardon. Sometimes I think High Command does that a-purpose to separate the sheep from the goats.

Last night four or five of us sat around the fireplace in the club shootin' the breeze about some of the incidents that happened back in the States. The best of all was the time that four of us were flying over Long Island. Below us we spot a light twin-engine Army ship cruising along, so we dive it one by one, and each of us does a barn roll around this ship. We zoom away and looking back we see that our prop-wash has flipped this ship over on its back. So we fly around for a while and land back at Farmingdale and laugh and laugh about it. But soon the phone rings in Operations and some Big Wheel wants to know who it was that buzzed a C-78 and flipped it upside down . . . on account of because it wuz a Staff plane and inside of it was highly upset Brigadier General. They never did nail the right people for that deal. Seems to me they pinned it on some jockeys from Norfolk . . . And then there was the time we buzzed Central Park; and the day we did steep turns around the Empire State building and waved at all the people inside. There were the many times we buzzed the Sound and caused various fishermen and socialite yachtsmen to leap wildly from their boats into the water. There was the time we buzzed so low that McKibben hit the water, ricocheted, and crashed in a little bay. I wuz sole witness to that one. There was the night my engine cut out and blew up over Mitchell Field and I had to set her down dead-stick and all covered with oil. Another gay night I buzzed Coney Island good and proper, and another night when I chased an observation ship in and out of the searchlight beams over NYC. There were the many minor accidents: the day that Ed Heller or Joe Gerst forgot to drop his tow target cable and dragged it (heavy rope with heavy lead weight on the end) thru the parking lot at the Republic plant . . . beat up forty cars, tearing hoods and tops off and smashing in their windows. Then he drags it thru a little wooden guard shanty and tears it down over the terrified sentry's head. The night Harker landed thru the hi-tension lines. The day I hit a snowbank and flipped over. The day Joe Gerst ran into three seagulls and busted his airplane all to hell . . . and so on into the night, reminiscing and popping corks at high speed.

The stove from which we removed the firebrick, having been red-hot ever since, is melting down gradually so we've been shopping around the field looking for a new one to swipe.

Set up a volleyball court outside the hut the other day and after the first flurry of violent activity all pilots retired to the lounge and their cases of ale. Liable to get hurt runnin' around after that stupid bladder ball.

Been sure feeling fine these days. Plenty healthy and rarin' to go. Not much in way of news to tell, for no recent adventures to orate about . . .

Chapter 10

· ·

Holidays at Bodney

Dec. 17, '43

J ust finished a rather poor letter, and had the thought that by the time
you monkeys receive it t'will be somewhere around Merrie Olde Exmas
time again. So before I let it slip my one-track mind, Merry Christmas
to ye. Now that that's done I kin rest easy. Say, by the way, if you uphold
the old tradition and roast up a fat turkey on that day, whittle off a chunk
of white meat and drench it with gravy. Slap a scoop of cranberry sauce
atop it, sniff it and savor it. Sigh, and then eat it. Do this at exactly 1300
hours and at that time I will smack me chops and choke down another
brussels sprout. Ho ho ho. Every time I go into our officer's mess I shut
me eyes until the orderly sets a plate before me. I open one eye then,
and peek. Goody! I scream. Spam, sprouts, creamed carrots that would
curl the whiskers off the toughest rabbit in England. Coffee that dissolves
the porcelain from the inside of the cup. (But boy does that stuff taste
fine about six a.m.) I get no fatter. I stay lean and get tougher and meaner
daily.

Every time the outfit flies combat, the ground crews and ground officers gather round the loudspeaker and listen in on our radio chatter. By
lending a careful ear, they can tell about how things are going with us over
the Continent. A lot of profane jabbering back and forth and it's a cinch
that things are poppin'. The other day I sat one out and heard the show
on the RT: "Hey!" some guy hollers. "Somebody come on down here and
help me out. I'm outta ammunition, six o'clock low on the bombers!" So

we back here on the lousy ground dance around and grin and wonder who it is. Anyway, when we are out operating over the Ruhr or elsewhere, the boys back home tune in and enjoy it as best they kin. When we land one by one or four abreast in tight formation in good weather we're met by a jeep that collects us up from our individual revetments. Back in the pilots' room we stand around and sweat out overdue ships. Then when all arrive who are going to arrive, we gather in the room and the intelligence officer (in our case, that appellation is strictly a misnomer) struts around getting various bits of military info from each pilot. What he saw and did, etc. How many chutes observed, etc.

Then out comes a quart or so of good scotch whiskey. Out with the cork, and the bottle passes around from pilot to pilot and we all get a couple of good jolts of lightning. Settles the gut and relaxes one from the high tension resulting from having been for a couple of hours in an extreme condition of alertness. Two hours of very hi-altitude combat flying leaves one in an abnormal condition, roughly. At 30,000 feet or better, one breathes short and fast, sucking oxygen for all he's worth. Any quick series of movements leaves one a bit pooped, shall we say. Sometimes I know up there when I start to say something over the radio, nothing comes out the first couple of tries, but a couple of unintelligible wheezes. At 35,000 feet a guy's voice sounds ragged and hoarse. Cold up that high, too. Around sixty below zero quite often. A human being at that height is quite the fish out of water. But I'll wager that with proper equipment (pressure cabin or pressure suit) I could milk this ship up to fifty thousand feet. Like to try that sometime.

Everybody seems to have gone to bed around here but me. And as this machine ain't conducive to quiet slumber I'd best fold up before I'm folded up. So for the second time tonight, good night . . .

Dec. 19, '43
Still I have nothing of great interest to spout about. Dismal climate for flying if ever I saw one. Like bad Long Island weather concentrated into one dense mess. Only one or two very light, damp snows so far this winter, but much frost and freezing mist. A dozen different cloud forms are always churning about the skies, and in general it's a flier's nightmare. Too bad they can't transplant some of Arizona's warm and sunny skies over here. Last night there was a heavy rain all night long, driven by a wind of gale velocity.

Tonight the stars are out again and tomorrow may bring some business.

Spent the past couple of days shooting much skeet, which involves blasting at clay pigeons and also at any sparrow, seagull, etc. that flitters past within range of our 12-guage flak battery. Some pistol shooting and stuff like that. Also some poker and rummy and a few small parties in the Club. By a small party I mean it is held in a small bar room, which is the only small thing involved. After months of effort, I finally hit the jackpot on our one thriving, thieving slot machine. It payed off five pounds. Friend Tom Colby and I, finding ourselves the sole survivors of last night's brawl, doped out a way to beat the one-arm bandit. We accidently broke the glass out of the damn thing and then spent a jolly time trying to catch the plums and lemons and bars when they came whirling around on the spinning reels. I awoke, not having bothered to undress, and found my pockets well-laden with shillings. So wandered around the field passing them out as souvenirs to one and all. The machine still owes me another five.

Have read everything I could lay hands on . . . Tale of Two Cities, Above Suspicion, Grand Hotel, Trout Fishing in New Zealand in Wartime, Five Weeks in a Balloon by Jules Verne, Pittsburg Post Gazette (Aug. 12th), two Colliers magazines of July and September, Pocket Webster Dictionary, The Case of the Counterfeit Eye, and A History of French Literature! Have also cleaned Capt. Gignac at countless checker games. This weather is drivin' us batty.

Tonight we made a toaster out of a coat hanger and grilled some cheese sandwiches on top of our stove. Our hut is quite a homey little jernt. Four feet away from the stove the temperature takes a slide down to around thirty-five or forty degrees, so we wear flying jackets and fur boots when not in close vicinity of the heater. Sometimes we even get a thin, high layer of alto-stratus cloud hovering about the ceiling. But we have a peachy time together. The other night Heller and I built a small fire on the floor to try to heat things up. We threw on old newspapers, etc., and eventually had a cozy roaring bonfire. McKibben decides things have gone far enough, and the more Ed and I bellered and laughed and hollered, the madder Mac got, so he grabs our pet fire extinguisher and pushes the control knob and puts out the fire with a quick squirt or two. But this is an odd extinguisher in that once it's started it runs until empty. So a generous stream of soda water wuz sprinkled about the floor, walls, doors, tables, bunks, clothes, etc. Those things sure work slick!

I have, in various moments of enforced idleness, done much figuring. (1) If we would chock our wheels and point all our ships due West and gun our engines, the combined propwash would blow this cockeyed island back across the drink where we could anchor it in Long Island Sound (2) Two million, four hundred thousand outboard engines latched onto the eastern shores would accomplish same (3) In fifteen flights to 30,000 feet, Northrop's engine must accomplish 18,000,000 more foot-pounds of work than mine, in that his large pear-shaped posterior weighs forty more pounds than mine. (He was highly teed off when I presented him with those statistics). (4) If we banked the corners of our perimeter taxi-strip, we could taxi our Thunderbolts lickety-split, without having to slow down for the turns.

Captain Gignac tells a droll story of fighting the war in New Guinea. When he wuz there they had no ice and so had to drink their beer warm. Until he began taking a case along with him in the cockpit every time he went up to altitude to intercept the Jap bombers. The beer would be thoroughly chilled by the time he landed again. Novel, that.

We often contend with winds of a hundred mph or more when flying at altitude. Amazing, ain't it? Would never know, tho, for we're just like trout swimming in a fast current. Do realize it, though, when we think in terms of ground speed. If flying downwind at 400 on the airspeed indicator, we then naturally cover 500 over the ground per hour. Which works out nicely if the tail wind is there upon our return from Germany, which it never is. Say, can you feature driving from Minneapolis to Chicago in an hour? Ol' tires would be smoking a little.

This intelligent letter will probably be your Christmas present. Ho ho ho! Ought to make it a more flowery article, but be switched if I kin think of anything to expound upon. Oh yes, our newly arrived "helpers," the P-38 Lightning pilots, have been insulting of late by saying that, by definition, "a Thunderbolt is a loud noise, causing no damage and followed closely by a streak of Lightning." #%!**!! Brother, they are just jealous, that's all I gotta say. Bunch of bums. Any jerk who would want to fly any ship with more than one engine ain't a pilot at heart. P-38 and bomber drivers are in the same class, and that's the worst insult I can think of at this time. One man in the crew, one engine, and one fan is all I want. A P-38 doing a barrel-roll looks to me like a bunch of kindling wood flopping around the sky. But what a slick, lovely clean aircraft are our Thunderbolts! Queen of the skies, no less. Clean bullet-shaped fuselage and clipped wings with a pleasing parabolic curve to 'em. A powerful radial in the nose, and the fastest job airborne. I wuz going to quit this letter after two pages, but I must make it clear in your minds about this thing that has come up. What a crowd of bums!

This has been a great day in our life. We got clean sheets for our bunks. Slept on the last for nine weeks. Sure choice things towards the end. Ritual for going to bed here is simple. First I lay all my fur-lined flying clothes atop the blankets in an even layer. Then as I peel off three or four layers of clothes, I spread them on top of the whole thing. Then I sneak into my cot carefully so as not to knock anything onto the floor. It's quite heavy to sleep under, but also very warm. Last night as I crept under the covers I met a beetle creeping out. He said, Ted, do you mind putting me on the floor so I can cuddle up to the stove? and I said quite all right, ol' boy, and did as he requested.

Life in the ETO reminds me of that old cowboy ballad, in part which goes, "... and the mice play shyly round me as I snuggle down to rest, and the board roof lets the howling blizzard in ..." Except we got tin roofs, which is different. Latest mousetrap to come out of the ETO is an effective one and plays upon the hungry mentality of British mice. A ruler is placed upon a table with one end of the ruler sticking out into space. A hunk of Spam is placed on the mid-air end of the ruler, and the thing is neatly balanced. A bucket of water is placed below the Spam. Mouse sees Spam, thinks it is food (!), trots out to get it, destroys the equilibrium of this machine, and is plunged into the water. The irony of this affair is that even should he navigate the course safely, all he would get to eat would be the Spam. And if you want to walk out on a teetering board to eat that, you deserve to drown. All have gone to bed and the fire dies down. Chilly climate in here so ... so long ...

Dec. 23, '43

Ah-ha. Have set sail on a couple of interesting cruises of late. One of which was to the farthest distance into Germany yet flown, I think. That was an interesting mission from beginning to end, for on the way out we ran into a tremendous black and glowering cloud. We meet this job about forty or fifty miles out to sea, and the whole outfit had to quit flying our beeline course and orbit around and around, climbing for altitude, to get over it . . . which used up quite a bit of my precious fuel. We finally strike out over the top, all of us laying long shiny contrails. We meet our bombers at the right time and place and give them a good penetration escort. There isn't much flak, and while we are with the Forts they are not much bothered by any snooping Hun fighters, and finally when we're all low on gas Colonel Joe Mason hollers on the RT: "OK gang, everybody out!" So most of our ships head for home, but four of us who happen to be the last flight lag behind doing another couple of sweeps over the Forts, and then we start for home.

But then we spot twelve disorganized contrails hiding in the sun, and by the very fact of their sloppy formation we see 'em and know they are Jerries waiting for us to leave our bombers. So Greene and Marshall and McKibben and I turn away from home and go lickety-split towards these bandits. They have a little altitude on us, and as we draw near them one Hun turns chicken and peels straight downward for home. Next thing I see are two Me-109s whizzing by me, a little to the right and a hundred feet straight over my cockpit and their guns are winking and blinking. Greene, in the lead of our four, makes a hard port turn and he and Al Marshall take out after these guys. Mac and I lose the other two of our flight so we stay upstairs and fence around with a half-dozen Jerry fighters. We can't afford to mix it up with them as we are right at the point of no return. Low on fuel, so finally we turn our tails to 'em and drive for England. (If they'd only known it, they had us cold meat at that point, ho ho!) The pair of us cut back on our throttles and begin to sweat out our gas. We get over Amsterdam finally, and then Mac sez to me, Hey, they're shootin' at us, Faro. And I look ahead and there parked some short distance off my nose are fourteen gobs of flak. We change course a bit and then there appears eight or ten jagged black gobs of smoke right between us, and we are not flying far apart. By then, tho, we are out over the North Sea so we start a gentle, fast let-down for home. We go down to four or five thousand feet and then down low to skim the waves, and boy they were some waves, and did that water look cold. We have a strong head wind all the way home and and that eats up more gas. (Later learned it to be a sixty-mile headwind). Finally after miles and miles of nothing but choppy green water my fuel warning light comes on, which means I have 15 or so minutes of gas left. So now I really begin to sweat, but at the right time we make landfall and the two of us set down at a big coastal bomber base. Mac runs outta gas while taxiing and mine is coughing. So we gas up, have a bite to eat, and then rat-race all the way home.

In the meanwhile, right after Greene and his wingman went chasing those '109s and Mac and I lost them, Greene and his partner go diving towards the Fatherland hot on the Huns' track. But another '109 dives on Marshall, gets on his tail, and begins to do a little fancy shooting. Marshall sees 20-mm shells busting and tracers going past his canopy and he hollers to Greene that he's being massacreed. So Greene does a stunt or two and ends up on this Jerry's tail, lets him have a couple of good bursts in the cockpit and down goes Jerry, smoke and flames. Chalk one up for Frank. So everybody finally gets home o.k., and what a day. Our group score is still better'n six for one, which ain't bad.

This same day, another squadron of our group was withdrawing after escort work was done, and they see a crippled Fort struggling for England. They also see five Jerry fighters making attack after attack on this pore straggler. So eight of our gang peel off to the rescue, and in the ensuing dogfight all five Huns were shot down for the loss of none of us! And after we'd landed, the same Fortress they'd saved flew over our field on its staggering way home, and was it shot up! Half the wing gone, two engines out, half the tail gone, etc. Quite a feat for her pilot.

We had a small party in the Club last night for no special occasion. Ed Heller, the mighty Irishman, is so mad that he's not had a decent shot at anything so far in this war that he hollers, I gotta hit somebody I just gotta! He trudges around the Club asking people if they mind if he hits 'em, just a small blow. He finds no takers. (Ed stands six-one or two or so and weighs a couple of hundred pounds . . .) Finally he tops off his drink and hauls off on a brick wall. A mighty blow, and he busts a little finger. Ho ho ho! A lot of sympathy from us he got, too.

Good movie tonight. The colonel tacked all our combat pictures together . . . enemy ships on the screen, twisting and turning and the image jiggles as the pilot fires his guns . . . tracers streaking out and blowing hunks of Jerry ships away . . . and now and then a shot in the right spot and the target disintegrates with a flash of flame.

All under control. Plenty to do most of the time, and with this jolly crew of pirates there's generally plenty mischief in the offing. Right now am heading for the Club for cuppa tea. Just one, and then to bed for I guess I'll fly tomorrow's mission . . .

Compared to his C-Flight mates, Ed Heller was a giant of a man.
He was displeased when he was compelled by his flight leader,
Frank Greene, to name his aircraft *Happy* after one of Snow
White's dwarfs. Heller finished the war with 5.5 aerial victories.

Dec. 26, '43

Well, howdy! With nothing any more lively to put into print today, I'll have
to tell you how Christmas was celebrated in this fog-stricken territory. The
day before Christmas the outfit flew to France on a successful escort run.
So I sat in the pilots' hut and sweat it out with ear glued to the radio re-
ceiver. Nothing more eventful than a couple of out-of-gas crash landings.
No shooting, so wasn't sorry to sit it out on the ground. All the ships of
our squadron got home o.k. and by then it was dark, on Christmas Eve.

Then a little before suppertime I walks out to my ship and met with
nothing but profanity from my crew chief. I find that an order has come
in from Fighter Command that an immediate change must be made on all
ships. New belly tank shackles or some such item, and the work will force
all of our ground crew to work all night long so the ships will be ready for
a scheduled Xmas-day mission. Something special the jerks at HQ have
cooked up. Well, naturally the boys moan about having to work all night

on this particular night, and especially since they have a party all lined up with great quantities of females and so on. It is sad, but c'est la guerre.

So the sun goes down and the wind comes up and the fog rolls in from the sea, and it begins to drizzle. And all the pilots have their dinner at the bar of the Officer's Club. Then the 486th pilots gather in our new pilots' room down on the flying line, for we have a small party arranged for ourselves. So I swipe four or five quarts of wine and wander down to my ship. It's cold as the devil and raining in gusts, and all around the field there are little lights blinking beneath our ships. When I find my ship there's a big Cletrack tug parked in front of it, giving the power for a searchlight. My crew is cussing away and working like mad, so I join 'em and tell 'em to hell with it for a while, and there we sit under the belly and wing of my ship pulling corks and passing the jugs around until way after midnight. Was really a nice party. Sat there under the belly of the ship swapping lies and working now and then, and after a couple of corks had been pulled nobody minded the cold wind at all. And when the colonel comes by to see how the work is progressing, he sees the pilot and crew of one ship laboring like slaves. But if he had he shoved his arm up into the turbo-supercharger, he'd have found three or four bottles hidden there.

So about four a.m. most of the ships are rigged and put to bed and then the crews joined their pilots in the hut and they got warm by the fireplace and proceeded to finish off the rest of wine and rum. But I swipe a jug of rum and make my way back to my ship where my crew chief is huddled and we have our own shindig. He sleeps all night out in the rain and I awaken in bed to find that my blouse has somehow disappeared. Some feller brings it in later, sez he found it in the middle of the airfields. Had a wunnerful evenin'.

Christmas the fog is thick enuf to cut and carry away in blocks, so back into bed we jump and snooze till noon. And we had a fine dinner… turkey with all the trimmings. It seems that one turkey had wandered away the previous evening, the evening of my under-wing party. Various amateur detectives cast grave suspicion upon me and Sgt. German, just because they found a pile of old chicken bones under my aircraft, the morning after. Circumstantial evidence. Some weasel or something drug 'em there.

Played some poker in the afternoon and wandered around to different huts saying howdy to various characters and having a nip or two with each. In the evening one of the mechanics knocks on the door and comes in with an armful of old Chicago papers for me, so I spend an hour catching up on the war news of the past couple of months. Sounds kind of tough over here!

So about the time we are ready to hit the hay, Pappy Gignac beats on the door with a club and reels in, full of liquid Xmas cheer. He keeps us all laughing for a couple of hours with his droll tales of skiing and flying. Gig's best story, tho, is the mournful telling of his bitter childhood days. He tells it with such a straight face, even in tears sometimes, that we almost believe him. About how when he was six years old and lived up on the Canadian border . . . his parents had left him on the doorstep of a small orphanage, wrapped up in a saddle blanket. And a year later he is adopted by some wicked French people. This man and his fat wife, they operate a little gambling house and they kept little Gig locked up in the cold attic, while they ran the Faro and Blackjack tables downstairs. They'd wake him at four every morning. Everybody would be drunk by then, and they'd whip him for sport and send him out into the woods, barefooted. And if he should refuse to go, they'd hold his little hands against the red-hot cookstove. Well, this went on for years, Gig says, until the Society for the Prevention of Cruelty to Dumb Animals finally got wind of it, and they rescued him. And then he ran away and joined a troupe of wandering jugglers, but as Gig sez, that's another story!

Right now, Gig is growing a fierce moustache, for his ground crew told him they were going to let their beards grow until he knocked down a Messerschmidt fighter, and they gave him orders to follow suit.

We got ahold of some popcorn last night, too. Leo's folks sent him some from Nebrasky, so we throw some of it into a mess kit and proceed to pop it atop our useful stove. Evidently this English fog has been working on this popcorn, for we sprinkle a layer on the bottom of the mess kit and heat it up good, with all the approved shaking and jiggling. Pretty soon the kernels start getting black, and they then start to squirm like things alive. Now and then one of 'em would go "phutt" and slowly spring open! Good for a laugh anyway.

So that was Christmas in the ETO. Wot a way to go!

Jan. 1, '44

You think you've had an easy winter. Well, it hasn't snowed yet over here enuf to stay on the ground, but I'll be hanged if the climate is worth the relatively warm winter. The temperature rarely goes below freezing, but the drizzle and eternal fog and low clouds are enuf to drive a guy nuts. Most of us are two-thirds cracked anyway.

Was scheduled to fly the combat trip this a.m. and was to lead a flight of four, but during the take-off I hit a rough part of the field and bust off the tail-end of my belly-tank . . . sprayed hi-octane for miles around and had to quit the formation and return to the field. Dive-bombed the field with the shell of the now-empty tank and then out of pure gleeful spirits I beat things up royally, dived and chandelled and dived again and buzzed across the field at two feet up and 350 mph, and carried on for a half-hour. (I knew that all the high-rank officers were en route to Germany at that time, so no one would be around to turn me in . . . ho ho.) Finished off my merry one-man air show with a climbing slow roll off the field and then landed and went out in a jeep to pick up the remnants of my belly tank. Lucky I didn't go on the mission anyway, for a lot of the boys came home short on gas and had to land and crash-land all over England. Again I say ho ho!

Jimmy Doolittle is our new boss over here now, and that guy ought to be able to dream up something wild for us to do in our spare time. Looks like the Big Wheels are getting squared away for a colossal fight pretty soon.

Cribbage board still holding up under the strain. We play the most cut-throat games you ever saw. Mostly four-handed. There hasn't been any poker of late, but we get paid tomorrow so something's bound to happen.

The first I heard of the flu epidemic in England was when you mentioned it in one of your letters. Guess I don't get around as much as I thought. I did ask the doc about it and he verified report. You don't see any of them pernicious leetle bugs on me or any of my flying buddies. This Scotch'll do anything.

Northrop crashed on the south coast today but was uninjured, happily. We have more cockeyed fun around here. I ain't had a close shave for two weeks or more and I'm getting bored stiff. You bet. Northrop, I might add, crashed pretty hard. Knocked him out for a spell, and when he comes to he takes his handy-dandy vest pocket-size screwdriver out and removes the clock from the instrument panel of his ship. Sez he knew it was up for salvage anyway and he hated to see some Limey get that chronometer. Leo is a collector at heart.

Listening to the RT today in the hut, and late in the mission we hear some guy holler, "There goes the s.o.b., I'm goin' after him!" And pretty soon over the radio we hear the thunder of eight fifty-caliber guns and then we hear, "Wow, I clobbered that bassard! Just like shootin' ducks!"

Don't know what you folks find confusing about the way I'm fighting this war. Simple. Bombers go out and bomb the daylights outta Germany. Us fighters protect the bombers to and from their targets. That's all it amounts to, nothin' to get confused over.

As for that drinking flask I asked you to try and find, no rush, but just that it might be a nice thing to carry around with all the rest of the junk I fly with.

As usual am keeping the boys awake with the typewriter, so will fold up for the night. Nice night, stars bright and a little hunk of moon riding high. Can hear the RAF boys plowing around upstairs, getting their formations in line for a night visit to Germany. Glad I fly in the daytime. No fun setting my ship down on a black night on a blacked-out field. No fun, but still interesting. Fun like hitting yourself on the head with a hammer. Feels so good when you quit.

Chapter 11

· ·

Winter Party Nights

Jan 2, '43

Sure spent a nifty New Year's Eve. We flew that day to some wild and woolly spot on the Bay of Biscay. St. Nazaire or some such. We pick up our bombers down there somewhere in murky weather and fetch 'em home to England. We are pretty short of fuel at this stage of the game and the weather is getting all loused up, so the gang of us set our wheels down on the long runways of a big coastal RAF airdrome. A few of the boys crash-land off in the countryside somewhere, unable to find anything better in the fog. We taxi over the grass, park our ships in a long line, and walk over to the control tower just in time to watch a delightful display of fireworks. There are a couple of bombers in trouble, so the RAF is shooting up big sky rockets and bombs that go way the hell up in the air and go boom with a big flash. Swoooooooooosh, and up goes a couple of very fine sky rockets. Pow! Wot a show. This display of pyrotechnics goes on for a while and then in came the bombers, a pair of 'em considerably riddled after a hard day bombing the Jerries. And as they clear the runway, in comes a tired old P-47 from a strange outfit, shot all to hell and much the worse for wear. Her bold pilot jumps out, pale and peaked, and proclaims that he's the sole survivor of flight of four which were attacked down over France somewhere. Lucky boy.

Well anyway, here we stand thinking of what a fine party we are going to miss at the home base, when up comes a lovely lass in the uniform of the WAAFs and she sez, "Come with me, Sirs" and we jump into a big bus and off we go with this frail at the controls. We dine in style at the RAF club (liver mit bacon) and then another babe drives us down to our billet, which is a large shack with a bunch of cots double-decked. We wash up a little bit and sit around laughing and hashing over the day's work, and then at eight-thirty another bus drives up and we pile in and are driven down to the Club.

It seems that there is a dandy party on tonight and we've all been invited. We look like a bunch of highwaymen, flying boots and coveralls and o.d. shirts and baggy pants. Not a necktie in the crowd. I have a dirty ol' silk scarf around me neck, and boy do we look crummy . . . here's all the RAF pilots slicked up fit to kill, and their ladies all in fancy evening gowns. Well, when we walk in we are met with open arms, and pretty soon everybody has a good buzz on. Thirty nurses are collected up and herded in for us to dance and neighbor with, and a bunch of stray WAAF officers come to the party, too. Say, we had a fine time! Plenty of scotch and plenty of good lager beer. Comes midnight and the New Year, and I'm playing ring-around-the-rosy with a RAF brigadier general! Comes the dawn and the sky is grey with fast moving scud-clouds, but into our ships we crawl and away we go heading for home.

A pleasant flight it was, too, skimming along about a hundred feet up, and England looked pretty unrolling under my wings. Buzzed over many little towns, all old and tired-looking, and over crooked canals and rivers and over low rolling hills and farms and over castles and estates now and then. Pretty soon we spot our field and down we go. I turn my ship back to Sgt. German with orders to fix a few gadgets that have gone haywire . . . oil spray on windshield, poor oxygen regulator, and so on. We get in just in time for chow, and by golly you know what we had? Toikey! Wit all the trimmin's. Wot a feed. This is the life.

Jan. 10, '44

Nothing red-hot to report today. Things going along same groove as of old. Weather pretty rough, and have an adventure concerning same to relate later on. Had an unusual opportunity to see a fine crash of a German heavy bomber the other day. The gang of us throttle-jockeys take the Forts in toward their target as far as we dared go with our limited fuel. We'd just left them and were re-organizing the squadrons for the trek home when out of the brilliant blue sky comes a lone Hun bomber. A Heinkel-177 long-range, crew of seven, well armed and capable of packing a terrific bomb load.

Well, this knucklehead barges right into the middle of our fifty-ship fighter formation, and we are so amazed at his crust that for a moment nothing at all happens. One of the other squadrons is available. We all pounce like a band of starving wolves, and it is a case of first come first served, and this other outfit gets there first. This bomber is at 25,000 feet and starts to dive and take fancy evasive action, but it doesn't do him much good. Pretty quick his rear turrets quit firing. There are about thirty ships queued up on him, taking their squirt and peeling away so the next guy can get in a shot. So a streamer of smoke trails out behind this big ship and down he goes, chopped to bits by our fifty-caliber stuff. We get in a big Lufberry circle and watch, and a couple of thousand feet off the deck the bomber explodes and falls in two parts in the woods. He explodes again with a tremendous blossom of red flame, starting forest fires. We catch a lot of flak over Le Havre on the way out, including some red-marker stuff.

Another day we flew a long escort job under very adverse weather conditions. Stuff they won't even taxi in back in the States. Our gang gets airborne and we plunk into the cloud base and start up thru. We lock in together, wingtip to wingtip, and make a tense but uneventful climb thru fifteen thousand feet of solid, turbulent cloud. This makes for very precise, difficult flying and requires utmost concentration by one and all. One tends to get tense and rattled and panicky now and then during a long blind climb, so each pilot has some secret formula of his own to keep his self relaxed on his controls. Some guys mutter to themselves, "relax relax relax relax, etc." Others whistle or sing. Me, I sang 17 verses of *Pistol Packin' Mama* into my oxygen mask on this climb this particular day. So finally we bust thru the top and into the bright blue sky and go about our business, which is shepherding a gang of Forts around over the old country for a while.

So then we start home again and close up tight for the dive thru that 15,000 feet of soup again. All goes well for a few moments. Major Richmond is leading the flight this time, with Northrop on his port wingtip and Mac on his starboard, with me on Mac's wingtip, and from my usual position of tail-end Charley I kin see the other three ships, all on my left, and the four of us are flying with our wingtips about six inches apart. Northrop's ship is only about thirty feet away from me, but it's almost invisible.

Just ahead of our four are four more, and eight more just behind us.

Down we go smoothly and with the greatest of precision. Then all of a quick things let go with a bang. We have drifted to a position squarely behind six other ships, and when their combined propeller turbulence hits us, our formation explodes and we all career violently at crazy angles. I spot Mac in his ship, perched up on one wing, and I see that I'm in a vertical bank on the other wing, and heading for an immediate collision. I think I'd best go elsewhere rapidly, so I roll over and gut the stick and presto! I'm all alone. I see a few dim blobs of P-47s flash past me close and then I'm alone, strictly. I'm now strapped into seven tons of aircraft that is immersed in the middle of three miles' thickness of pea soup. I now go on instruments exclusively and work for a while to get ship under control. Finally the needle and ball center and I commence a nice 200-mph letdown. Then I glance up and notice a quarter inch of loose dirt piled up on the glass OVER my head. By this oddity I gather that I've been flying inverted for some time. Ho ho. So I roll her over am so elated to be right-side-up that I proceed to get careless. Next thing I know the stick beats back and forth and I'm spinning. So I cast an eye to the altimeter. 19,000 feet and unwinding rapidly. I decide to bail out at 12,000 if still spinning. But I recover from this quaint maneuver and settle down to business, flying in a large circle while I steady my nerves and turn on my gyro instruments. I find a hole, finally, where I can see down thru a long tunnel and I dive down and come on home on the treetops. When I get back over the field, the visibility is about a quarter-mile and people are shooting rockets and stuff to mark the runway, so I land o.k. and breath fifteen or twenty fat sighs of relief. Wot a show. Stuff like that there sure breaks the monotony. Old Higgins had a close one the same day. He spun out during the climb up and recovered from his dive 200 feet off the ground and clocking around 500.

When I lurch into the pilots' hut for that shot of whiskey, I tell the boys about my unconscious inverted letdown on instruments, and cries of disbelief fill the room. But most of these jockeys have learned to fly only with gyro instruments, or have concentrated only on that method of blind flight. On the other hand, I've always mistrusted an artificial horizon in fighter planes, and have spent many many hours recovering from odd positions with use only of needle-ball-air-speed, and I'm pretty good at it. And so that theory of mine paid off today, as is proven by the fact that I sit here telling about it. And as for not knowing that one's head is aimed earthward, that is a common sensation. We're strapped in tightly, and upside down is all the same as right-side up. Makes no difference. And to save my world-wide reputation for veracity, Major Meyer of 487 Squadron phoned our boss, Richmond, right after he landed, to tell him excitedly that he'd just spun out of the soup and made an inverted let-down, unknowingly.

Letter today from Bill Cunningham. He's over here, a soldat in an engineer outfit. Wrote him, and trying to learn his location so we can get together some evening.

You oughta hear the rain beating down on our tin roof tonight. Glad I'm fightin' a gents war, where one gets his dirty work done and returns to a life of comfort and waits till the next session. That mud and rain and sloppin' around in same ain't for me.

Haven't been off the field since that grueling 10 days in London with Willie O. and Mac. Whew. Content to spend my days prowling around the field, poking around the ship, and playing cards with the boys. But the food gets rather monotonous. Spam for lunch and corned willy for dinner, or vice versa. When I hit the States, it's a dainty diet of raw steak and shrimp cocktails.

We're all biding our time and waiting for spring and summer when we can fly every day or twice a day, with none of these dull days of sitting around to endure.

Jan. 11, '44

Since I got some colored wax pencils from home, for a joke, I guess, for Christmas, just to show who the joke is on I enclose a couple of fine portraits I just now painted. These here pictures are far from finished jobs indeed, but perhaps by examining them close-like you can make out what a fighter pilot in the ETO looks like.

Flew a couple of hours non-operational today, just zipping around doing what I pleased . . . pulled some dandy buzz jobs on local airdromes and bounced a couple of Limey bombers. Lot of fun and a chance to polish up on some stunts I thunk up one night while deep inside a beer mug.

Good movie tonight. Assignment in Brittany . . . lots of action and some fancy bow and arrow shootin' by a commando who plunked arrows into several Nazi sentries with great ease and skill.

Weather looks fair tonight . . . broken clouds with the moon showing thru the cracks. Might be some flying to do tomorrow, so best I get a little snooze. A three-hour trip upstairs leaves us pretty well bushed, for it's a lot of work to fly this onion at thirty-thousand feet. So, Guten abend . . .

Jan. 17, '44

Ain't much in the way of excitement at this stage of the game . . . fog has been so thick in this neck of the woods that they've even given the seagulls two-day leaves. Might be something cooking tomorrow, I hope. This sittin' around give me the willies.

A scene of peace and quiet in this mangy hut tonight . . . Leo lays on his bunk playing Clementine full blast on his Jews-harp. Ed and Mac and Joe and MacKean are bunched around the stove reading old Sat. Eve. Posts . . . Archy and Greene are off on a five-day leave. The bunch of us are just finished playing a dozen games of cribbage. A wee bit of rain is now swishing onto our tin roof. Right now Leo got a laugh out of us by imitating the sound of Jerry jamming our radio. Sounds so realistic that I think Leo has discovered the way the Supreme Command does it. But I s'pose they call their machine by another name.

A letter from Russ Craig the other day, mailed the first of January from Sardinia. Figures on being home at Easter, but he failed to say which Easter. Russ sez that life is rather monotonous and he wishes he were flying my ship instead of operating his low, slow target.

Puttered all day. Filled out my log book, which I'd neglected for six months. Whipped Pappy Gignac a couple of games of checkers . . . Gig's new moustache has sprouted red hairs in all directions.

Going to London soon and will pick up a pair of flying boots I spotted last time in town.

Half the time nobody knows what the day might be, or the date or indeed sometimes even what month it is. Odd situation.

None of the gang is infected with English talk yet. A hot mission is still hot mission, and not a "good show" or a "wizard prang." A ship is still a ship and not an aircrawft. Etc.

Northrop is now toasting a chicken leg on top of the stove. Where he got the chicken leg no one knows. He can always find something to eat somewhere. He hides various choice tidbits under his pillow, in one of his shoes, under his hat, etc. Then when he gets to a point of starvation every night about eleven, out comes a ham sandwich or an egg or a plate of cold beans. Beats us how the guy can eat so constantly. Wot a character!

Jan. 20, '44

Letter from Tommy telling of his recent exploit. Head-on collision with another Thunderbolt. Kills the major in the other ship and rips Tommy's ship to shreds, dumps him into thin air, opens his chute for him, etc. And spends an hour or so in Chesapeake Bay in winter-time, when normal people would croak after a quarter hour. Lucky to get away with it. Luck plays a good part in this racket. Some guys got it, and some ain't. Tom and I have a surplus, so we don't need to bother much about anything connected with flying these hacks. Hope to see Tom over here before long. If we ever get into the same outfit there'll be hell to pay.

Was pretty slow going for a few weeks, but today the weather broke and we got in a little mission. Most enjoyable, but no encounter with Jerry fighters. Weather's too much for the Luftwaffe.

All they did today was throw up a bunch of flak. Big black puffs all around at times, but those jerks ain't very good shots.

Leaving in a couple of days for ten days detached service. Willie O. Jackson, McKibben, and I. Will be situated quite close to London and we aim to have some fun out of the deal. Amounts to more or less of a flak-farm setup, only we'll have some hot jobs to fly around in when we please. May get a chance to check out in a Spit.

Glad you had a nice Christmas. We didn't do badly over here, either. But not much to spout about these days. Last couple of weeks have been deadly monotonous for lack of action. Went into Cambridge with Leo the other evening, but transportation is so excruciatingly dismal that the trip is definitely not worthwhile. The poor dinky overworked English trains are just barely wheezing down the wavey tracks. A terrible thing to behold.

Jan 27, '44

At this stage of the game am situated somewhere in lower London town. Been here now for about five days with Willie O. Jackson and McKibben. I think we are supposed to be attending some specialized flying course at a nearby RAF fighter airdrome, could be a gunnery affair or something, I dunno and care less. We three took off from home with our P-47s bound for this RAF base at Woodchurch or Hornchurch or some such odd name.

We get to the edge of London where this place is, and the fog closed in. We navigate around like mad for a long time, catching glimpses of rivers and boats and factories but never an airfield. But we finally spot it and it's a crooked, dog-legged runway, grass field, and we barrel in and set down in a red-hot fighter-type landing. With skill and precision, that is. Real good, like. So there's a bewhiskered old gent, a RAF Squadron Leader, who meets us. "Where's the gunnery school, Mac?" we ask, polite-like. Well, he didn't rightly know and we didn't ask further. Our orders read ten days gunnery school, and being so close to London town we can't see going home and telling folks we couldn't find what we set out for. So Willie O., who is leading our trio, suggests we goof off into town and lay low for this ten days. Well, he talked Mac and me into it, after some arguing of course. And five days have passed now, I think, and after five more, at least another five-day leave will be required for us to recover from this hot-dog expedition. Mon dieu.

We've seen some shows . . . took in that very peachy one called "Good Night Ladies," and a rowdy affair indeed. Willie said we took it in, anyway.

This London seems to grow on me. Have enjoyed sauntering around the back streets, poking thru old shops (wine) and along old lanes (en route to more olde shoppes).

And I must leave you now, for it's pub-time.

Feb. 1, '43

Howdy do? Back from London, and sure good to be in with a bunch of white men again. Missed a rare session of fine flying weather, during which the mob got a good bag of aerial combat victories. Doggone, sure missed the fun that time. And now that I'm back, of course, a quilt of fog has covered the field, effectively putting our pets to bed for a while. We've given our meteorologist twenty-four hours to straighten out 'ol Man Weather. After that, time is up and if things are still bad, up to the highest limb he goes to dance on this misty air for a while.

Had a French lesson this afternoon up in the squadron hut. A learned Corporal in the squadron was our professor. A comical affair it was, too. We have a list of the phrases and words most valuable to us should we bail out over France and attempt escape back to England. And if a pilot can make big talk with the peasants, it makes escape just that more simple. So our class gets under way. Right off, Archy wants to know things. He growls, "How the hell do you get 'wee' out of 'oui'?" He claims it ought to be pronounced Oy. And so on down the list. I have a beautiful picture of Archy and some nifty wench from Paris trying to get along together! (They say that U.S. parachutes, of the finest silk, are much in demand amongst the young ladies of France. Rumor has it that many a French lass —alas, if one could but verify it!—wears silken panties with U.S. Army Air Corps stamped across the tightest-fitting section.)

I flew my ship down to London on this ten-day deal, so I let Mac fly it home and I came on home with our ground crews (who were also included in on the deal). I did the navigation from the front cockpit of a jeep, using an aerial map for a road map, and it was a chore trying to find the way over the tenuous little lanes with only main routes and landmarks shown on my charts. Came up thru some extremely scenic countryside and we had a helluva time. Called a halt to the convoy about noontime when I spied a wee thatch-roofed inn along the road, wherein we irrigated our parched throats with many a pint of light ale.

Have had a few warmish days, but always it goes back to a chilly drizzle. Spring will be welcomed by this gang, but we understand that Summer comes on a Wednesday this year, over here.

P.S. Got into a pretty noisy air-raid in London while there. Lot of fireworks. Picked up a couple chunks of flak from the streets for souvenirs.

Feb. 2, '44
What a jolly evening this is. You bet. Wuzn't much to do the first part of the night. Read a couple of dandy comic books and an old Pittsburg newspaper and some of Archie's letters. Then I walked in circles, dodging two other gentlemen who were walking some circles in a counter-clockwise direction. Then I suggest to Mac that we go over to the club and have a drink or two or three. We hook down a couple of beers, play a game of cribbage, and get a canteen filled with half Port and half Sherry wine for 15 shillings, and then we proceed to the mess-hall kitchen and make off with a big chunk of bread and some bologny and one fat bermuda onion. So back to the hut we go and build us some lovely sandwiches. I stick mine on my hunting knife and cook it a while on the stove. I eat it. It is choice indeed. I wash the last crumb down my hatch with a long gurgle of wine. Then I light up a cigarette and now I'm batting away at this infernal machine.

Weather being lousy, we shot some skeet this p.m., and much sport. I got 85 out of 100 clay pigeons, plus one real pigeon and three sparrows that were going home on the deck and flew thru our flack zone without taking the proper evasive action. We had a guy—speaking of flak—the other day in the outfit who did the same. Enclosed find clipping telling his sad story. As it was in his case, all turned out happily and he didn't even catch cold from his unplanned swim in the cold North Sea. By the way, now numbered amongst the countless items we carry in our parachute dinghy is one of them there little heat-pads . . . When one finds himself boating in the cold Channel, he just whips out this little job and dumps a little water in it and he has himself a small-time heating system over which to thaw out.

While I think of it, that London is sure a hot town. About twenty thousand American soldiers in town all the time. Milling around. Mostly airmen. Mac and I have told each other countless times that when we go in we'll go on one of these sight-seeing tours and see all there is to see. All the famous things, things of culture, etc.

Well, when were there on this ten-day deal, it occurred to us again. We arranged for tickets at the Red Cross Club and traipsed on down to where the bus left from. There's a forty-year-old bus alright, and parked outside a dingy place. Ah ha, we say, this is the place where we acquire some of this culture. So we go inside to get our tickets and there sit a bunch of old ladies waiting for the bus to leave. A bunch of old ladies drinking TEA! We case this rugged situation at one glance, and with one mind we beat a hasty retreat and scamper down the lane to the closest bar. Which effort is the closest we have gotten so far to being tourists. Hell, we've seen all the stuff. There's a swell bar down a little alley near Trafalger Square. There's another swank jernt down on Piccadilly Street near Old Bond Street the Rivoli Bar of the Ritz Hotel, where Mac and I get to telling Lord Beaverbrook's son how to run this here war just the other day. There's a nifty dance hall near Charing Cross Circus and the notorious Regent Palais bar is just off Piccadilly. At five-thirty every evening that bar is stuffed with used fighter-pilots. And one or two B-type gals. Good scotch, too. We have seen Hyde Park, for that is where one finds the Marble Arch, which in turn is a fine place to make rendezvous with the babe. Big landmark. Cawn't miss it!

I even saw the shop where they made Big Ben, too. Got lost one day trying to follow a Bobby's instructions as to where one might find Liverpool Station. I wandered thru some crooked alleys and there it was. I synchronized my watch with a little model of Big Ben. Gee. Wuz I havin' fun.

So now I retire. Weather bad in the morning, sleep til nine. Weather good, up at dawn. Phooey. Arizona, here I come. Too bad we ain't fightin' the Mexicans. Boy, would we build up the flying time!! Say, that gives me an idea . . .

Feb. 4, '43

Had wonderful day yesterday. Went out with the boys and we ran into some weather. Climbing up thru several strata of clouds was seized with an extreme case of dirty ol' Vertigo (complete loss of senses of position, direction, and flying altitude of your ship, etc., caused by general confusion of inner ear, vision, etc.)

I was flying contact with Mac's ship, meaning flying visual tight formation on his ship while he flies the instruments. And the first thing I know I'm looking up thru the top of my canopy at his ship. I couldn't dope out whether he was inverted or whether I was the guy who'd gotten upside down. Found out soon enuf when I stalled and spun out. Spun a half turn left and a half turn right and recovered on instruments in the clouds. By now I'd lost sight of the squadron so I struck out alone on the original course and climbed up again, coming out four or five miles behind the mob. Caught up with them finally. Then just inside the German border my engine cut out and by the time I had that running again I was way below the gang and had used up too much fuel during my chase. So I radioed to Mac that I was going home alone. He didn't have to escort me back as I'd fly back on the gauges inside the cloud layer.

So off I go merrily. But now I see a lone Fortress also heading for home, so I strike up an acquaintance with him and proceed to give escort, flying circles around him and playing thusly for a while. So I take him out to sea and halfway home and then leave him and go on alone. I decide to buzz the water so I go down through eight or ten thousand feet of cloud, on instruments, and then find I'm icing up badly: I pick up a half inch of ice on wings and gun barrels, and it's forming so fast I can see it building up deeper and deeper. Mm-hmm, I think. Gotta do somethin' or else. I can't climb up thru the icing strata, so I dive down to 200 feet where I break out the bottom of the clouds and buzz the water until the warmer air cleans the ice away. And I proceed on home to work the field over with a buzz job. A most entertaining flight, and I learned a lot about flying. Didn't think the ice had me worried, but upon landing I found myself spitting blood, for I'd chewed a couple of holes in my cheeks where I'd sucked 'em in and bit hard . . .

Today was perfect, however. Ship ran like a dream and the job ran off without a hitch. Mac and I flew with Willie O. today, a major now, and he leads a smooth flight. A fine pilot he is, and plenty aggressive. We looked for trouble today and doggoned if we could find any. Got a kick out of landing after the mission. We land practically at the same time, four of us abreast but stay staggered back a bit. Anyway, I came in on the final turn into the field, wheels and flaps down, and Mac was on my left. I had a bit of speed on him so I slid on past him, about ten feet away, and both of us clocking 120 mph. So I wave at him he waves madly back and I holler at him on the RT to get the hell going, so he gives 'er a little soup and we land at the same time and practically at the same place. A nice formation landing always makes us happy. The simple things in life . . .

No matter what you may read in the fancy reports in Chicago papers about the ferocity of aerial battles over Europe, leave us not fret a bit about me or any of the gents in this squadron. We've been selected as fighter pilots and with these ships, guns, and our fine teamwork we can take care of any opposition. We take care of the bombers as best we can and at the same time cover one another with the greatest of glee. A fighter pilot can't get himself blasted if he is not surprised, so naturally we develop beautiful individual and mutual cross-cover. We cover one another's tails and each pilot watches out for his own hide, too. You couldn't any more sneak up on us when we're in formation than you could march a platoon of hobnailed troopers thru an old maids home without wakin' 'em up.

Letter from Bill Cunningham today. He's up in Wales now, wading around in mud he sez . . . Bloody old Wales he calls it! The Limey atmosphere has got him already. He hates English beer, as we all do . . . but I note that we keep on drinking it.

The outfit feels a 100% better every evening after we've flown three or four hours during the day. Food and drink to us. A week on the ground and we're grade-A material for the psycho ward. Walk in circles and then sit, steeped in gloom. Then walk in circles the other way and sit spitting at each other. But tonight everyone is all smiles and jokes agin.

We were just now trying to think of the meteorologist's name. He's a lieutenant who's been with us for months and has done good work for us, too, but no seems to know his name. We all call him Stormy! He takes quite a beating. Every night at supper somebody will holler at him, Hey Stormy, how's it look for tomorrow? And he'll go into a lengthy discussion of fronts and clouds and winds aloft and more technical terms and end up by adding, "It'll probably rain, though . . . " Ho ho ho. What a character.

Enuf of this continued story. The more I fly this ship the more in love with 'er I get. Lovely hunk of machinery. Lovely. Could go on for hours, but I won't . . . so long . . .

Feb. 9, '44

Not much news the censors would pass, but have had a swell week of it. Flown five peachy missions in a row and feel like a million bucks. Seen plenty of action, but none of it thru my own gunsight, worse luck. Wot a ship. She goes like a scalded cat up thar in the stratosphere. (I scalded one yesterday just to see how fast a scalded cat really went, and they go pretty good.)

I have here in front of me a clipping out of the Providence Evening Bulletin. I will copy it verbatim on account of because it is so rare. First I'll copy it and then pick it to shreds. I quote:

SNOW WHITE'S PILOT GETS SEVEN
DWARVES SAFELY HOME
Capt. F.N. Greene, Riverside, Downs Attacking Nazi

Capt. Franklyn Nathaniel Greene of Riverside flies a P-47 Thunderbolt fighter plane from an 8th AF fighter station in England. He has named his ship "Snow White."

As a flight leader, he commands a formation of eight planes; his own and seven others. The others are, of course, the Seven Dwarves.

Recently the flight had completed its part in escorting a number of heavy bombers to their target in Germany. Capt. Greene and his men headed for home at 30,000 feet, flying comfortably with the sun at their backs. Another mission completed, and not a German fighter in sight.

Suddenly one of the Dwarves broke the serenity of the flight by shouting over the inter-plane radio: "Holy Cow! Look below!"

About 1,000 feet down, the Americans saw 12 Me-109 fighters, tightly packed, obviously looking for action. "Snow White" and the "Seven Dwarfs" were outnumbered three to two, but they tilted over in a dive and went down together.

The heavy Thunderbolts dropped into the middle of the swastika-marked planes. The Germans split into two groups of six in an effort to trap the P-47 fighters.

Immediately Capt. Greene became wary(!) He didn't like the look of things and was about to tell his men to "hit the deck" when one of the Dwarves shouted, "Frankie, I'm being attacked from the rear!"

Capt. Greene whipped his fast-moving P-47 around and pointed its nose for the '109 that was maneuvering for a shot at the Dwarf.

The image of the German grew in the faintly illuminated circle of his sight. He touched the trigger. Streams of .50-caliber slugs from his eight wing guns hit the German plane. The '109 disintegrated as if it had been made of match-wood. After that, "Snow White" led the "Seven Dwarves" home to their base in England."

Wow! What a thrill! We have laughed and bellered at this article for a week now. I think some dame back in the cocktail lounge in the States wrote it up! I ought to know, on account of I wuz there. Let me correct it on a few points . . .

First off, Franky-boy only got six dwarves—I having refused to partake in such a name for my ship. And then in the second paragraph where it sez we wuz flyin' home comfortably at 30 grand with the sun at our backs: We wuz up there that high, allright, but brother that ain't comfortable, physically or mentally. For like they say, "Watch the sun, it hides the Hun!" (fundamental surprise attack in anybody's air force is to hide in the sun and come out of it shootin').

So we come out of the old country, a'headin' for home, with the sun at our backs and we are lookin' backwards plenty. And we see those dozen '109s trying to hide in the sun. But they aren't below us, but above, which gives them the delightful advantage of altitude, which means speed, and which gives them the edge on us by all rules (error no. 3). They wuz massing for attack so we did an about-face and went for them, to take the initiative, which counts. And by the way, the remark over the radio when we spotted 'em was not "Holy Cow, look below!" It was "Jeeeeezus, Greene! There's ten o' the bastards, six o'clock high in the sun!" (error 4 in our Providence account).

So next thing I see is two '109s scooting past over my head and quite close, close enuf to see the rivets in their wings. In the melee immediately following, the four of us (not eight as in the report) get split up. Mac and I are together, and Greene and Marshall are together. Greene shoots a '109 off his partner's tail. The latter had hollered not "Save me, I'm being attacked from the rear," but "Somebody get this bastard off me arse!"

So then Fran and Marshal skeedaddle for home. In the meanwhile, Mac and me wuz all alone and lonely, having lost our other two in the deep blue skies. So we head for home alone, turning our tails to six-plus bandits who are still up-sun of us. We couldn't stay and play becuz we were very low on petrol, like they say. For some reason or other, the remaining Jerries failed to attack us. They had us cold if they'd known it. (errors five, six, etc.). And again, I say, I ain't no dwarf. I rebelled, refusing to name such a beautiful hunk of machinery after a cockeyed dwarf. Just ain't right, I figgers. And furthermore, Greene didn't bring his gnomes home safely. Mac and me brung ourselves home safely.

And speaking of names for ships, I have a Joker out of a deck of poker cards glued onto my Mae West for a silent partner. Might paint a big joker on the nose of my ship and call 'er that!

Have 46 sorties now, but don't start thinking about seeing my ugly face in the States for soon. We'll be over here until they don't need us anymore. Things are coming to a focus I think, and also I think that leaves out the States, for fighter pilots will be nil until the Nazzys decide to turn in their chips. Which is allright by me, for I kind of hate to leave now that I've got my teeth into the thing. However, like some Frenchman said when he didn't know much about anything, "Que sais je?" which means I dunno.

Well and happy, and sure hope you home folks are likewise. The fire in our little stove has gone out and the fog has rolled in and it's so cold in this durned hut that right now I kin hardly wiggle me toes. So will snooze til sunup . . .

Chapter 12

. . . .

Loony Birds

Been a pretty fair week over in the ETO. Enuf flyin' to keep the bunch of us outta mischief, but still not as much as we'd like to see. We figger that when the big day comes, we'll be ahootin' and flying and strafing and dive-bombing all day long, from dawn til sundown. The Thunder-bomber is quite an innovation! But as of now, we mostly scour the thin air of the stratosphere looking for trouble in the form of any Luftwaffe jockey who has the crust to stick his nose up that high.

Frank got his DFC the other day, complete with hi-falutin' ceremony, and since then has been hard to live with. Leo swiped the thing and put it between two slices of stale bread and gave it to Frank, suggesting he try eating it inferring that after the war he'll probably have to. The gadget consists of a bronze maltese cross with a four-bladed prop superimposed, and all dangling from a colorful strip of ribbon.

A fighter squadron, you know, is split into three flights of eight pilots per each. And so in our own, all the violent shaking, tilting, and whirling of our own private set of sieves has resulted in a sorting-out of personalities with each flight somehow acquiring its own brand of people. So A-Flight has a bunch of old wimmen pilots, Sunday drivers, if you know what I mean. On the ground, anyway, conservative and business-like. B-Flight a mixture of Sunday drivers and some guys a bit more on the carefree side. But C-Flight (mine!) has not a brain in the lot of 'em. Loony birds, diamonds-in-the-rough, rugged individualists from way back. Would just as

143

soon be here as anywhere. And our little bunch is perhaps more closely knit that the other flights, for we're all survivors of the original bunch of the Fightin' 21st. Replacements are absorbed into B and A flights, while C-flight remains intact. Like they say, birds of a feather etcetera.

Been spending our evenings hashing things over in the Club, as usual. Talk revolves around flying, mistakes made in same, tactics, unusual incidents, and so on thru the night . . .

Feb. 21, '44

Pretty good day . . . logged me some more combat time and had a nice peaceful view of a lot of fighters and bomber, all ours.

Old buddy Frank Cutler is back in the outfit again, after a month or so with Jerry command. Glad to have him back, and he's really back with a vengeance. He did some beautiful shooting yesterday. We made rendezvous with bombers at 25,000 feet over Germany and intercepted 30 or so Jerry fighters and had a running gun fight for a half hour. Ol' Frank clobbers two '109s and gets a '110 on the ground on the way home. We got twelve destroyed in the air with loss of none. One ship of ours scrapped upon landing due to combat damage, but pilot intact.

Swore to the boys tonight that I heard crickets creeking outside, and when I invited them out to listen to'em, they went, and hearing nothing at all decided I'd finally made the turn. Guess it was nothing but my ear being full of air, or not full of air as the case may be, from the altitude today. I hope. They don't often block up, but have a slight head cold which may have done the dirty work.

Some of the boys got into a scrap today, getting four more '109s for loss of none. Saw a few B-24s spin in, with a few chutes appearing at intervals. And on the way home Cutler, MacKean, and Marshall break out of the Dutch coast near Egmond, and they spot a flak-boat just as it shoots down a strange P-47. So the boys peel off on this E-boat, set up a traffic pattern, and strafe the hell out of it, silencing its guns, killing its crew, and leaving said flak-boat burning and sinking.

Had some snow the other day, in squalls, and the only snow I've seen over here that stays on the ground is a thick blanket of same which now covers the rolling country of Germany. Must be pretty miserable in their bombed-out cities in this bitter weather. Methinks that their misery is just beginning.

Flew a thousand miles between lunch and supper today, and in about the length of time it takes you landlubbers to get down to the Loop and back. Zip. Play that one on yer pyano.

Sky clear tonight and maybe some business tomorrow . . . You want to know what to send me, eh? Well how about some blue sky with no clouds therein. Also could use a large bagful of hot weather . . .

Feb. 22, '44

Easy day. Slept late and did nothing thereafter. Took a couple-mile walk this afternoon and spent the evening in the Club drinking beer with the mob. There was a war correspondent around this evening talking with the boys who've been doing all the shooting of late. Got to neighboring with this bird, Ernest Byfield by name, also of Chicago, and find that I went to school with his son, E. Byfield, Jr. We were all a little fried and gave this geezer a helluva pack of lies.

Wish summer would come so I could get out of my long-johns. Have two pairs and I wear one pair until folks start avoiding me. Then all I have to do is to take a shower without removing them. Simplicity itself. I saw a mouse run out of my flannel shirt this morning as I picked it up off the floor to put it on. I think he sleeps in it nightly. Every night after the lights are put out, we kin hear the mouse jamboree. They dash about the room hollering "WEEK WEEK WEEK" at each other.

We have other playmates, too. The flying field is the stomping ground for some three hundred thousand seagulls, and every time we take off they swish about over and under us and seem to revel in allowing themselves to be swirled about in our prop-wash. Not bad hitting them at speeds below 150, but hit one doing 350 or so and they put a turrible hole in one's ship . . . as though a cannonball had hit.

Feb. 27, '44

Our style has been slightly cramped by the mists that periodically shroud the moors in these parts, but this had been a fair to middlin' month for action. Fly two and then sit one out. A pain in the neck. Gets to be a habit: look at the flying schedule to see if you're on the mission. If not, the next step is to walk over to the Operations officer (Willie O. Jackson) and curse him roundly. Then bitch and trudge around working yourself into a rage. Then watch the boys get into ships and race away, leaving you to sit before the fire listening to the fun being piped in over the radio.

By the way, in last weeks' Yank magazine we noted a letter written in by a couple of soldiers (chairborne, no doubt) who signed themselves, "G.I. Bible Discussion Group." Their sad cry was that no hells or damns be allowed in print in Army literature! Ain't that a hot one? I never heard of such crap. We all wished they listen in on our radio chatter during a mission. You ought to hear (or rather ought not to) some gent in the outfit holler when his belly-tank fails to release . . . or hear him speak when an oil line develops a leak over Germany! Ho ho, 'tis comical indeed to hear some of the remarks that come thru the earphones. The Great White Father better shove a cloud in his ear if he frowns upon such chatter.

Last trip over, on a deep penetration, sure saw some fine country. One little town in particular caught my eye . . . there was a long snaky river winding thru some snow-covered mountains, and in one bend I saw this pretty village with thick forest starting right in the back streets, and it looked just a sketch out of a fairy story. I imagine that there weren't any soldiers at all billeted in that town and that life there was pretty much the same as it had always been. There were only about fifty houses and a shop section on three sides of the village square. The fourth side of the square sided on the river, cobblestones sloping down to the water . . . a few small docks and a few little boats. Quite picturesque (maybe not too accurate a description, as it was studied for ten seconds from four miles up at 400 mph, and besides, I was pretty busy watching out that some furriner didn't sneak up on me and cut loose with his shootin' irons, etc.). But we do manage to sneak some looks at the country we fly over. In one mission I guess our eyes cover more square miles of Europe than half the Europeans know exist . . .

Speaking of looking at country, I'll tell you some of what happened to four of the boys. On the way home from Germany one fine day, they flew above an overcast for what seemed a very long time. So down they come thru the cloud deck to look over the lay of the land. Ah-ha, they cry over the radio to one another (and we back in the pilots' hut can hear 'em): "England! Leave us find a field and gas up!" So right down to the deck they go and fly merrily along over the hedgerows. But one pilot hollers, "Too goddam many windmills to suit me!" and another voice tells him, "Hell, they got windmills in England!" But soon another voice sez, "Hey mac, that's about the tenth goddam dike we've hopped over . . . " and the same optimist answers, "Well, quit bitchin. They got a lotta dikes in England, too!"

Pretty soon one pilot sees that his altimeter registers about twenty feet *below* sea-level. He lets out a holler about that, too. But then the flight of four fighters buzzes up over a small town, and over a field where they notice a platoon of soldiers drilling. These soldiers immediately go hogwild and run off in all directions and right away a lot of smoke trails from tracer bullets criss-cross in front of the ships. Which clinches the growing suspicion in the minds of our daring aeronauts that this ain't England at all. So they leave Holland for the Dutchmen and head out across the North Sea, bound for friendly territory, flying low and slow and using hope instead of hi-octane fuel, of which they have almost none. Two crash-land in shallow water off the English coast and two limp into coastal airdromes, running out of gas while taxiing. What a very, very daring thing to do . . .

Also remind me to tell you one day of Black Friday in The Hague. (No herring . . .) MacKean, Heller, and Pappy Gignac were responsible . . .

Couple of days ago Mac and I get into our ships, off duty, and embark upon a mischief-seeking low-level flight. A helluva time we have, and we scared more Englishmen than were scared during the Battle of Britain . . . which is a few.

Chapter 13

. . . .

Meeting the Mustang

Mar. 7, '44

An interesting week, this last one. A few long missions. Longer indeed than could ever be flown with a Thunderbolt! So I'll settle down to explaining that last puzzling remark, and the enclosed clippings will amplify. Take special note of the one telling of the Mustangs (P-51s) taking the bombers right over their target at Berlin! They flew over five hours, or perhaps 1,800 miles nonstop, which is quite a trek in a single-engine pea-shooter. Well, ol' Ted was along for the ride, and here's how it came about.

Late the other afternoon we're sittin' around the pilots' hut drinkin' ale and shootin' the breeze, as usual. There's a whine in the sky and I go out for a looksee, and six of these sleek little Mustangs come sputterin' in for a landing and taxi up to the 486th flight line. First time I ever saw one, and it registers as being a clean little machine. Well, Willie O. up and sez, "Who wants to check-out in one of 'em?" Me! I hollers, running for my 'chute. So I crawl into the tiny little cockpit and Willie O. shows me how to start the engine. This is an in-line engine and I never sat behind one before. He sez, Well Faro, think you kin fly 'er? And I sez, Better get off the wing Willie cause here goes nuthin'. So all the boys come outside and stand around to watch the fun. I taxi out and she feels mighty strange after that big damn barrel-chested P-47. But she feels good, too, and I give 'er the needle and am airborne before I know what the hell has happened. I make no turns, but climb just a little at high speed, straight out from the field and all the time I'm hunting around the cockpit for the gadget to pull to retract the landing gear. I am some twenty miles from the field before I find it, and then she really starts to get out and go. I take her upstairs and fall in love with her. I rack around thru some chandelles and she's full of fire. I slow-roll and barrel-roll and then I meet up with Willie O., who has taken off in another one, and we fly thru some stunts in tight formation, and then I bring her in for a landing. So I'm number one in the whole outfit to fly this Mustang, and I log 35 minutes of P-51 time. And the boys give me the razz for takin' off and flying over the horizon with my wheels still dangling. But I tell 'em I couldn't find the levers.

So comes the dawn this a.m. and a mission is called, target Berlin, and the weather over our field is lousy as usual. Dirty low-hanging thick black overcast. And at briefing it is decided that the 486th Squadron will fly 16 P-47s and 7 P-51s, the latter to carry on escort beyond the fuel range of the Thunderbolts! So the few of us who had checked out the evening before get the honor of flying these new fighters. We make up a little seven-ship squadron, with Willie O. leading, and Pappy and me, and a couple of more of the boys. None of us have over a half-hour in the cockeyed thing, but we are so eager we kin hardly wait.

Off we go, and our formation is pretty jerky, for this ship is exceedingly sensitive in response to controls, but we square away and close in tight, break away from the 50-Thunderbolt formation, and we zip up into the overcast and have a few highly nervous minutes until we break out on top. And the rest of the outfit is having bad trouble somewhere down in the ten-thousand foot layer of heavy cloud. The radio is full of frantic chatter for a while, and it isn't until I get home five hours later that I find out what happens, and it has happened to my squadron. But that is another story, and I'll tell it later in this letter.

We get up to altitude and learn much about the Mustang in a short time. She's tricky and nervous up there, but we're doing o.k. for a bunch of amateurs. So we escort along with the '47s and when they turn back for home somewhere just inside the German border, the seven of us bore on ahead of the bombers. We're at 28,000 feet when Pappy spots a couple of '109s way down below, and they are shooting the hell out of a crippled B-17. Tally-ho, he hollers, and peels off vertically downward. I, nacherly, am tail-end Charley of this flight, and when I roll over to follow 'em down I haul back on the stick, as of Thunderbolt days. But I have failed to empty the rear internal fuel tank—eighty gallons and located right behind my armor-plated armchair. So with my center-of-gravity so far to the rear, when I gut the stick I go into a dandy hi-speed stall and skitter off across the skies for a spell. When I recover control and peel off again, the fight down below is all over. Pappy has shot down one of bandits and the other has gone home, and the B-17 is safe. It is shot all to hell, so we escort it to the Zuider Zee and then go home and land. We land, jump out, and look at our fellow pilots and their P-47s with scorn, and they regard us with awe and envy, which is as it all should be.

So then I find out about the trouble after take-off. The squadron of sixteen '47s was squared away for the long climb thru the overcast: a tight formation of four flights of four ships each, with flights in trail. They bore up into the soup, climbing fast on instruments. One of the boys in the lead flight gets a bad case of vertigo, loses his position, and slips back squarely into the middle of a tight flight of three ships. So four Thunderbolts tangle up in a ball, thusly bringing our most vivid fears of instrument formation work to a sharp focus. My ol' partner McKibben is involved, and he finds himself at 3,500 feet in the soup, dressed up in half an airplane, so he dumps the canopy and bails out. One ship spins in, killing the pilot, Lt. Earl Bond. One of the other three pilots comes churning out of the bottom of the overcast low to the ground directly over a large bomber base, where he landed what was left of his Thunderbolt. Mac, in the meanwhile, is dangling head-to-the-ground beneath his parachute, for his feet are fouled up in the shroud lines. He lands on his head and his hands in the backyard garden of an English home. So he picks himself up and is counting his arms and legs when the lady of the house comes out and calls to him, and I quote: "Hello, Yank! Would you like a cup of tea?" and that's the pure truth, believe it or not and so help me! Like a joke in the New Yorker!! Well Mac sez he went into a fit of laffing that liked to've killed him. He was picked up shortly and taken over to a bomber base, where they fed him well on scotch-and-soda until he got back to normal!

So tonight in the Club we have a helluva party, with all the boys pouring medicinal whiskey into Mac at a great rate. His eyes are neatly blacked and his hands and faces scratched up considerably, but he's lucky. He wuz laughing and tellin' the story of this typical English hospitality over and over, and each time he'd laugh harder.

So I thank the little Mustang for having me aboard today. Any other time I'd have been in the middle of that rat-race in the clouds. Ain't I the lucky one?

Before dark Archy and I took a couple of these P-51s out on a volunteer rescue mission, just the pair of us. For it seems that great quantities of B-24s were crippled over the target and low on gas, too, and have gone down in the North Sea. So we cruise fifty miles out to sea, orbit around, and transmit for a "fix." Then the Limey ground station vectors us to various locations. We're in radio contact with the Air-Sea Rescue speedboats and with the ground controller, too. We spot a dinghy and direct a rescue launch towards it. It's sort of monotonous work, sweeping back and forth on a search for a tiny dot in the water, but when you think that the dot consists of a half-dozen fellow Yank airmen, you sure strain your eyes. After a big raid there are always a bunch of Forts and Libs plopping into the briny deep, with their crews scrambling out of the rough, icy water and into their rubber rafts. And this Air-Sea Rescue outfit does a land-office business fishing them out.

This evening when Archy and I are out hunting the boys out, we run into a rescue launch and try to guide it to this raft. There are low clouds scudding the waters, and Archy tries to tell the Englishmen on the surface how to turn so as to contact the raft. The speedboat misses the raft and Archy tells 'em on the radio: "Hello Seagull, make a 180!" which means turn around and head the other way. No savvy. Archy repeats and repeats, frantically. No savvy for a while, and then one of the Limeys in the boat comes back at us, and his tone is one of sudden comprehension: "Hello Yanks! You mean *come about!*" Hell, we ain't sailors. You don't come about in a Mustang. And I guess you don't make a 180 in a speedboat.

Now and then of late we've had days that feel almost like Spring . . . warm sun and cool breezes with clear skies. CAVU stuff (ceiling and visibility unlimited, to you). But the nights are bitter cold. Take me back to Phoenix . . .

The 486th squadron threw a dandy party last Saturday night. Been planned for a month or so, and Frank Greene was the big operator. He had us all chip in three pounds for this load of Scotch whiskey he said he had lined up. Ten cases of it. He was to fly up to Scotland in our Norseman plane and haul it back. Well, Saturday comes around and no wheesky, so the flight surgeon comes thru with two gallons of medicinal alcohol (!) and he and Willie O. Jackson make up a batch of punch with grapefruit

"People back home keep asking me, 'Ted, how many fellows does your plane carry?' Which makes me madder'n hell on account of anyone knows that a fighter carries one guy, and it takes a shoehorn to get anybody over 150 pounds into the cockpit of this mighty Mustang. A unique thing about this snapshot is that the aircraft is clear but the pilot is blurred, and the moral is: steer clear of alcohol and grapefruit juice."

juice for flavoring. We have our pilots' hut fixed all up fancy, with a jukebox and polished floors and blue lights and big fire in the fireplace . . . looks just like a ritzy roadhouse! Where the hell the juke box came from I don't know. So a bunch of nurses come up from a local hospital and there are a dozen queens up from Cambridge, who have been invited en masse by various eager lads. There is a phony French countess and her partner up from London. This countess runs an elite bottle-club in a cubbyhole off St. Martin's Lane in Soho. A character. So by midnite there is not a drop left of our Kickapoo Joy Juice. What a punch! Delicious and refreshing, but it's a good thing there wasn't a mission the next day. The party is terrific.

When C-Flight gets back to hut that night, all hell breaks loose. Northrop, who is logging a little dual, wants the lights out, so Greene and I shoot 'em out with our .45s. Then I spot a big jar of talcum powder on a shelf over Leo's bunk, and while Archy holds a flashlight spot on it, I settle back and take a long, steady bead on it and pull the trigger. Talcum all over, like a burst of white flak, and Leo is not happy. I run outta the hut laughing and Leo empties his .45 in the general direction of my cot and I count seven shots and return to find my mattress smoldering and my shoes perforated here and there. It all sounds like a gun battle in a western movie and is hilarious sport. Our ground officer neighbors in nearby huts were quite terrified, we found out the next morning. One cringing soul even went so far as to dash for the air-raid shelter when the guns started popping at three a.m . . . Ho ho ho. Next morning MacKean and Leo and I spent a couple of hours sticking corks into the 24 bullet holes in our tin roof and concealing the evidence with adhesive tape. Boy do we have the fun, tho.

Have also had a time of it beating up the airdrome with our new ships . . . buzzing across the flight line at 400 mph and pulling straight for a mile or two vertically, just showing off. That Packard Rolls-Royce Merlin is quite a chunk of engine. Sort of hate to part company with my dear ol' Pratt and Whitney radial, though . . . Can't beat that one for dependability under all circumstances.

Our Intelligence Officer has made up individual combat flight records for us, with mission summaries of all trips across the drink. Make a good souvenir. Think I'll go out this p.m. and take some snapshots of my ship and crew. The film has been damp for eight or nine months now and may be no good. Wish I had a good color-camera here, would take it along on some of these missions and get some swell shots of our formations over the scenery: contrails and flak, etc.

Speaking of the latter, we flew over a particularly heavily defended area some time ago and I spent a half hour taking violent evasive action trying to keep out of clusters of flak bursts. Tom Colby and I were coming out alone and they concentrated on us, and it was sort of fun in a quaint way, for I put on a regular ol' air-show . . . Immelman turns and loops with quarter rolls and everything I could think of, and all the way around I could hear the dull bloomp-bloomp-bloomp of bursting shells, and I was rather uneasy for a while. Bet the performance had the Jerries on the ground flak positions standing around their mouths open. Their conversation probably went something like this . . . "Achtung! Thunderbolt! Ready—Aim—Fire! Missed him that time, Hans . . . Wow! Lookit that guy go . . . Wow, he's gone nuts . . . Bang bang bang . . . Fritz, you led him too much that time . . . Wow, lookit him go now . . . Wow, bang bang bang bang . . . Wow right behind him . . . Wheee, lookit him fly that airplane!"

Flak doesn't bother us at all, for we can and do take peachy evasive action that throws off the aim of their automatic deluxe flak guns. Matter of fact, we get a charge out of watchin' them fire heavy-caliber shells up at us at a fee to the Jerry taxpayers of about a thousand bucks a shot.

Mar. 8, '44
Joe Gerst got a clipping in the mail today that I'd like to copy off for a souvenir:

U.S. THUNDERBOLT RULES AS
WAR'S PURSUIT QUEEN
Plane Once Hailed as Ungainly Now Hailed as
Fighter- Bomber-Strafer
— BY WES GALLAGHER, AP STAFF WRITER

LONDON, FEB 15: The ugly duckling is quite a warbird in the skies over Europe today. The P-47 Thunderbolt, that ungainly child of American engineering genius, once criticized as too fat, too heavy, and too much for one man to handle, today challenges the Spitfires for the title of pursuit queen of the skies.

Their tails used to come off during test flights (he's telling us!), but since going into action in Europe they've shot the tails off 657 Nazi planes against a loss of 186, to compile one of the most remarkable air records of the war.

During the past six weeks, P-47s have been fighting hundreds of miles over unfriendly territory and have shot down 223 German planes for a loss of 49 American.

Not since the Battle of Britain has such a lopsided score been compiled. Two years ago American fighters were the most controversial weapons of the war. The now obsolete P-40 and the Airacobras failed to impress as pursuit craft. Then came the Lightnings, and Mustangs, and finally the P-47 arrived, and she's compiled the best fighter record of the lot.

P-47s designed for high-altitude work are equipped with turbo-superchargers . . . However, in the ETO playful Thunderbolt fighter pilots returning from escort missions that had been dull scooted down and started shooting up trains, trucks, and airdromes in Germany . . . found the great firepower and heavy armor of the Thunderbolts made a formidable strafing weapon . . . Their pilots are also now carrying bombs.

Unquote.

Another small clipping:

U.S. BOMBERS BLAST HOLLAND'S NAZI BASE.
Important Airdrome Struck in Drive to Weaken Luftwaffe.
LONDON. FEB. 14: American P-47 fighter-bombers took over the offensive to whittle down GAF strength today with a smash at Gilze-Rijen airdrome, one of the Nazis' main fighter bases in Holland, executing the swift attack without loss. The Thunderbolts carried bombs instead of reserve fuel tanks to heavily defended Gilze Rijen field 65 miles inland from the Dutch coast. The assault was carried out so rapidly that not a single German plane took the sky in challenge.

Dat's all. (But I don't think any of us hit anything worth hitting!)

Them good ol' '47s. What a ship. Wish I could buzz the house one day, one of them good buzz-jobs that sucks the windows right of the joint with the low-level speed of it. Like to take this gang down Michigan Boulevard and thru the slot between the Tribune tower and the Wrigley building. Wheee.

March 11, '44

Howdy! What a dull week. That's a lie! It's been wild and woolly from start to finish! Have flown both Mustang and Thunderbolt on trouble-making expeditions all over occupied Europe and deep into the Reich itself. More durned fun. Have had numerous bouts with flak, and have lost most of what little respect I ever had for it. They're sure lousy shots. Have fallen as much in love with my Mustang as I ever was with that bulldog P-47.

Recently, in a half hour or so, I did more flying than I've done in the past six months. Here's how it came about, and to hell with the censors:

About six-thirty a.m. today there was called a Group Pilot's Briefing, which was surprising since the field was buried in fog and the clouds were on the ground. So the Colonel asks for 36 volunteers for a risky trip. Well, we all want to go along, so the squadron commanders pick out twelve pilots apiece and the others are asked to leave. We are briefed for a low-level attack on three airdromes in Pas de Calais—Abbeville being the 486th Squadron's target. (Pas de Calais is notoriously the most heavily defended of all German-held territory: it's the stretch of French coast across the Straits of Dover from Dover, England. It's the coastline where the Jerries sit with their fingers on the ol' trigger, sweating out the invasion . . .) And it is fairly obvious to us that our High Command wants a bit of firsthand poop on the area. So our briefing consists of planning a surprise attack: we take off and hug the treetops across England, flying as low as possible so Jerry radar can't pick us up. Then we plan to buzz down the Straits of Dover, parallel to the French coast and a half dozen miles offshore. At a signal, the three squadrons will fan out abreast, make a ninety-degree turn, and barrel in, up, and over the enemy cliffs, whereupon we hedgehop inland to our targets. And we're all flying Thunderbolts this trip.

So I damn soon find myself skimming the choppy waters of the Channel, getting salt-spray on my windshield, for the waves are just a few feet beneath us and the ragged clouds are just a few feet above my canopy. I'm at one end of long line-abreast string of 36 ships, and they look mighty mean, all bobbing and jerking up and down slightly, for it's difficult flying in that little slot between waves and clouds. We dump our belly tanks at a signal and I see them splash and bounce behind the other ships. We make our complicated swing towards the coast, en masse, and we're en route to hostile country. It's all a big secret we think, but then in front of us we see many white plumes of water spout up, which is shellfire from the cliff gun batteries.

So I pull up over a cliff and head into the thick of it and soon find myself clocking plenty of mph in a crazy twisting-and-turning buzz job. As you no doubt know, a buzz job is a zero altitude situation wherein, if you find yourself looking down at the tops of the trees, you get back down to where you'll stay healthy. And that level is about 3½ feet above the local terrain. Some call it "contour-flying" and the British call it "rhubarb-raiding," but I call it one helluva fancy buzzing.

So the instant we barrel up over the cliff, things go all to hell and it's every man for himself. The country is hilly and the tops of the hills are in the low-hanging clouds and it's a case of jerking the ship up a hillside into the soup, counting one, two, three and pushing the stick forward and hoping you're over the hill. Off to my right I see a Thunderbolt explode and hit the ground. But we try to bore inland individually. The Jerries cut loose at me with rifles, shotguns, water-pistols, bofors-guns, 88-mm guns, rocks, bricks, light and heavy machine-guns, old shoes, etc. I never knew before that I could fly with such skill and precision. Had everything up to the firewall (wide-open throttle and never got above ten or fifteen feet . . . under hi-tension lines and telephone wires, etc.)

About this point, the squadron leader hollers, "Everybody out!" and I suppose each pilot thereupon tried as hard as I did to retreat back to the Channel. I couldn't turn around, for the bastards with their flak kept herding me inland. Saw many amusing things (not counting the tracers weaving their shiny trails around my cockpit!) Flew down a narrow gulch and when I spotted the 20-mm shells exploding on the bank beside me, I cruised thru a city to get away from the fancy shooting. I think it was Amiens or Abbeville. Flew right down the main street at the first-story level. Shops and houses and stuff going by lickety-split, to say the least. People dashing madly about . . . wonder I didn't lop off a few heads with my prop. Then out the other end of town with tracers chasing me, and a skidding turn around a church-steeple and there's a machine-gun nest in the steeple and they clobber me when I go past. I consider coming back and blasting same, but don't dare to pull up for the turn. So up another valley. Came up over a timbered hill and out across a plowed field . . . couple of peasants cultivating with a two-horse team, which immediately went hog-wild when I went by . . . last I saw of it, the team was reared up, and the two farmers were hanging onto their cultivator for dear life. Over the river and thru the woods . . . came upon a farmer perched atop a haystack. When I emerged from the forest heading straight at him, he takes a graceful nose dive and huddles at the bottom of the stack . . . went by him about ten feet away and he sure was terrified . . . I could count the hairs in his whiskers . . . felt sorry for the old boy. Many farmers would wave back at me when I went by 'em, but a lot would just crouch by a road and stare. I would wave at one and all . . . friend of the people, that's me. Headed for a gap in a wooded hill and when I saw it was too narrow for my wings to fit thru I went on thru up on edge, sidewise. And so forth, to add up to one of the damndest flying jobs I've ever pulled off. Did a little shooting too, and seemed able to hit things I aimed at. Much haze and low clouds, too.

So pretty soon I approach the coast and barrel down thru a kind of gully that led to the beach, and then I was over the water again and happy to be there. I figgered myself to be the sole survivor, thinking that nobody could fly as crazy and crooked as I'd done and get away with it. But I see a few tattered Thunderbolts emerge from the cliffs and then I see a '47, about mid-Channel, stagger around and then the pilot bails out into the water. So I fly on back home alone and land, and I get out and sit on the grass and have a smoke while I ponder the devious ways of life. My propeller is stained green on all blades, from chopping through the weeds and grain fields of La Belle France. And I discover that my kidneys have functioned somewhere along the line, without orders from me. So, hi ho, I'm on the ground and we wait a while and count noses.

Of our 36, three are down in Pas de Calais, one is in the Channel, one has crash-landed at Manston on the English coast and eight more are riddled with flak—three to the extent of being scrapped. My ship has only a couple of little holes in it, plus a small tree branch stuffed into the airscoop.

We tuned in on Lord Haw-Haw this evening over at the club. The jackass is still braying with a smooth and convincing line of chatter. He tries deftly to disrupt Anglo-American unity and Anglo-Russian unity. Tonight he claimed the recent American "terror-raids" on Berlin had not cut German fighter production at all . . . went on to make reckless claims about U.S. raid losses over Germany. One point he brought out tonight, which could possibly have some sense to it, was that bombing tends to strengthen the will of people, rather than to break it. German bombing of English cities did more or less serve to temper their will to fight it out, but then again, methinks, Jerries aren't Englishmen.

Nights still cold, but days getting warmer and noticeably longer now. Have sweated out some pretty tough bad-weather flying of late. I think that any one of us would rather face the entire Luftwaffe single-handedly than to auger around in some of the soup we've flown in. Rough stuff in a fast fighter.

Hope everybody at home is well and happy, for I sure am. Scant chance for a 30-day leave in the States until we polish off them Nazzys. They still have a lot of fight left in 'em, so don't get ideas out of the local papers as to when the war'll be over!

When the Invasion does start, we'll be a busy bunch of boys . . .

Mar. 14, '44

Been operating Mustangs and Thunderbolts indiscriminately, and one's as good as the other. But each has certain qualities the other lacks. If you know what I mean. (Can explain in greater detail when I kin talk without looking furtively over my shoulder . . .) Love the '47 because she sure can dish it out and take it. Love the Mustang because she's a regular lil' ol' peashooter . . . small and shaped like a sharp-nosed bullet, and when I get strapped into her tiny cockpit that ship really feels like a part of me. Advantages and disadvantages to each. However, they're both stick-and-rudder and throttle jobs, and that's all I need for plenty of fun.

We've got the Jerries howlin' mad these days. No matter which way they turn we plaster 'em with a stick of fat bombs, and follow our bombers up with a string of grade-A fighters which proceed to blast anything left over. Also, everything in the line of opposition is being cleared outta the skies. It's give and take, of course, but we lose one fighter in the day's work and Jerry loses ten. But we can stand the losses and they can't. Their fighter production is pretty well crippled up now, and they can't replace their lost ships the way we can.

I don't think the Huns get a kick out of meeting us in the sky, fighter to fighter, the way we do meeting them. Look at the enclosed snapshot of the ace Nazi throttle jockey. Ho! Looks pretty bad off. Ol' vulture sittin' on the vertical fin of his ship.

Sure want to bring some of the boys out to the house some day. You'd like 'em all. McKibben in particular. "Imp" is the best word I kin find to describe the guy. Talk about a mischievous gleam in the eye, he has it. Oh me, what a gatherin' we'll have one fine day around the 'ole homestead! Will expound in a later letter about the merits of these dead-end types of C-Flight.

Last night Greene got to talking in his sleep and he hollers, "Well, we're at 25,000 feet, you know!" A while back Ed Heller mumbles in his sleep . . . "There's three bandits over there, let's go get 'em!" And last night I dreamed that I was conducting a solo sweep over Holland and shot the wings right off'n a FW-190. So I land beside the wreckage and take movies of the Jerry pilot as he climbs outta the splinters. So, you see that we fly twenty-four hours a day, and we ain't no Sunday pilots, either, on account of we fly in all weather day or night, anytime and anywhere, all for three bills a month. But we'd any of us do the job for nix, for we sure do like our work.

How's the little Nash running? Be careful driving that iron around . . . whenever I get into a jeep with someone else driving and they go over 30 mph, I get the heebie jeebies! Them things ain't safe . . . you can't back your turns and the road ain't a thousand miles wide, like mine is. And also you run up against a bunch of numbskulls operating their machines in a highly sloppy manner, while I run up against a gang of top-skilled and carefully reckless operators who know how to cut a fine edge, knowing the angles so as to make what appears to be a daredevil incident really be only a precise maneuver. See wot I mean?

You must be all grown up now, Toots. Come to think of it, I haven't seen much of you for the past couple of years or so. I ain't changed much at all . . . me hair was already sort of a dirty grey, so this business won't show up there. My face ain't sunburned, for when I do see the sun I'm flying. Nobody ever sees it from the ground in England, and many natives here don't believe there is one. But over the clouds my puss is covered with helmet, goggles and oxygen mask. I ain't gained any weight, but neither have I lost any. I haven't grown any taller or shorter, but all my clothes and uniforms have shrunk, due to violent English dry cleaning, thusly giving to the casual observer the impression that I am clad in hand-me-downs. I have taken to 100-octane for dry cleaning purposes as well as flying. Wear moccasins when I fly and on ground except when on leave. Ain't seen a necktie in months, but wear a greasy dirty silk scarf wrapped around my neck and tucked into shirt front. Comfortable, that's us. We let our hair grow for months and our beards until they itch too badly under the oxygen mask. Get a lot of sleep and loaf around a lot, but when we do get into our ships, we pack more action into a couple of hours than a pencil pusher sees in a lifetime. Wot a life!!

As usual I'm the last one up, so I gotta stoke the damn fire and turn out the lights. So long and love to one and all . . .

Mar. 20, '44

Will proceed to look thru your letters and answer any plaintive questions posed therein. Have no head cold . . . none for two months or so, for some reason or other. (Probably due to the 3-ounce shot of scotch which the

Doc doles out to us after each and every combat flight. There ain't a germ known to medical science that can survive a swim in good scotch whiskey . . .) Glad you liked the hasty cartoons I sent a while back. Manage to chalk one on our blackboard now and then. Last one showed Archy paddling a rubber dinghy over the waves of the Channel, with a signboard pointing "40 Miles to Dover," stuff like that there. My new jacket is called a battle-jacket. Non-regulation, but we manage to get away with it. Have to dress for dinner around here of late (order from some fathead in London HQ), so the jacket saves wear and tear on my good blouse. Stuff it into the cockpit sometimes when flying a mission we know will end up at some other base overnight, so then can wander into town for an evening. Now and then end up at some RAF 'drome near one of those old resort towns on the south coast, so like to drift into town to see wot's cooking.

Have taken some snapshots lately and it'll be some time before they get back from 8th Air Force censors who do all the developing. But the other day we all had to dress up for some presentation-of-medals ceremony, so after that was done we took some pictures of the pilots in a squadron bunch. Will send 'em home. C-Flight, as usual, was laughing and probably all you'll be able to see will be front teeth. We have more durned fun!

Am taking a five-day leave with McKibben at the end of this month . . . probably go to London. They (Jerry) manage to drop a couple of fat bombs down that way every other night or so lately, I watched two pretty good raids last time I was there.

Spring is slowly coming our way, by the looks of things. Every other day is sunny for an hour or so! Temperature must average around 45 or 50. Haven't removed my long-handled woolies yet! Matter of fact, they got so aromatic lately that tonight I had to break down and wash 'em out . . . two pairs of 'em. Got them hanging on a chair close to the stove now, trying to dry them out by morning. Also washed out three silk scarves: Rocky and Mac and I matched pennies to see who'd get the chore, and I naturally lost.

See that you now get two gallons of petrol per week nowadays: two gallons will just about get my engine started. Matter of fact it takes about twenty gallons to warm the ship up and taxi out to take-off position. Under quite a bit of throttle she burns two gallons per minute, and that's about as fast as you ladies could pour it out of a bucket! So you see, with all that kind of stuff going in a thousand planes all flying at once, we need gasoline like mad. And so you gotta be happy with just a squirt in your tanks now and then. C'est la guerre. And by the way, what feeble answer does Joan have in reply to that blizzard which raged thru Los Angeles a while back? Hmmmmm? Ho ho ho!

So Toots is putting on some wight, hey? (That's Limey for weight). Tell her not to worry about a trifle like that. I am far and away the scrawniest gent in the squadron and it doesn't bother me one whit. For a fact, it gives me a better rate-of-climb!! I tell the boys that I only got one corpuscle left, and then go into great detail telling of his wild adventures as he scrambles around the bends in veins and arteries. Much joking goes on every cockeyed day about that pore corpuscle of mine . . . how he hides in my cigarette lighter to keep warm when I'm flying in 60-below zero weather at thirty-thousand feet . . . how he dislikes bitter English beer and jumps out onto the bar whenever I take a drink, to keep from becoming paralyzed! One day I put in a formal request for the Flight Surgeon to make a search of all the local blood banks to see if he couldn't locate a pretty brunette gal corpuscle to keep mine company during the long winter evenings.

Happy to see that you're taking in the long-hair musical stuff lately. Ha-ha! I'll take Spike Jones and his City-slickers any day. And by the way, all this hullabaloo of late about hill-billy music becoming so popular . . . hell's bells, I've known that for 24 years . . . . Ol' Roy Acuff on the sad ballades . . . Birmingham Jail . . . Blood on the Highway . . . Take me Back to Tulsa . . . Jeez.

Wouldn't plan on a visit from me quite yet! That old business of flying a tour of duty of 200 hours combat and then going home for a while is quite passé these days. I believe now that a "tour" is as long as military necessity calls for . . . and it won't be too long before every pilot in the ETO will be needed plenty bad, to give air support to the invasion forces. Wot a busy bunch of butterflies we'll be then. Plenty of whoopin' and hollerin' and shootin' . . .

By the way, that vertigo business I wrote of is a common thing. Not a sickness, but just a general confusion of one's balancing apparatus (ears, inside) that tries to speak lies into one's brain when one's plane is flying inside of a cloud. All thru our flight training we've learned to forget the instinctive signals that this balancing apparatus in our ears relays to our brains. Absolutely must discount that sensation of turning when flying on instruments. And must only concentrate on and believe in what your flight instruments indicate.

Sometimes in instrument flying, your natural feelings of balance and position can lie to you, whereas your gyro instruments will tell you your exact attitude. All a pilot has to do is believe them. The other day Greene and McKibben and I flew up thru 10,000 feet of cloud. Greene, in that case, flew the instruments for us all while Mac and I—one on each side of Greene—flew visual formation with him. We three are making a straight-ahead climb at a constant speed and a constant rate-of-climb. Pretty soon I notice Mac's ship jockeying up and down violently, and I laugh ha ha ha and say to myself . . . pore ol' Mac's got vertigo! But then I swear I see Greene roll his ship up into a steep bank, and I feel that I'm turning to the left. But I steal a look at my gyro horizon on my own instrument panel, and it shows nothing but a straight-ahead climb . . . Wow, I say to myself . . . things are rapidly becoming confusing again! Then I cut loose and begin to tense up and jockey my throttle and controls. There are the three of us, appearing to be suspended motionless in a grey void, except for our relative motion to each other. No ground in sight . . . no sky and no nothing but a directionless, horizonless soup (typical view inside of a cloud bank . . .) Mac is hopping all around in an effort to stick with Greene, and I, to a lesser extent, am doing likewise. Finally, I talk myself into believing that we actually are proceeding normally, and I settle back down to business. That day I wuz not only doing imaginary right and left turns, but I was also inverted for a while—in my own addled mind!

We seldom get this vertigo business if we are flying on our own instruments, for then you are concentrating solely on your instrument panel with no outside influences, and can readily believe the story that their combined gyrations tell. That's simple to do (when you know how) . . . matter of fact, I like to fly instruments, but when it's a matter of military flying— taking fifty ships up thru an overcast and having to keep them all together in tight formations, while the pore wing men have to fly a tight visual formation up thru the soup—then it's rough duty. However, we take 'em up thru most every time we fly out on course, so it gets to be routine work. Always good for a sweat on the coldest days.

Last night I unzipped my B-4 bag to get out a pair of shorts, and as I pawed thru the towels and sox, a big fat mouse hopped out and ran around my bunk. Find mice in the oddest places around here. Leo found out the other day that a whole gang of 'em had set up housekeeping inside his footlocker—having et their way thru the rear corner of it. Pore chubby Leo . . . he hides various goodies away behind his bunk, under his mattress, in his footlocker, etc., so when the pangs of hunger strike him (which they do every half-hour or so) he can just reach around a corner and pull out a drumstick . . . but we sometimes get there first, and if not, the mice gobble them up for sure. Get a bang out of Northrop. We call him "B-B," which is short for Bubble-Butt. Quite a character. He's of about the same general proportions as a bubble once he gets into all his flying paraphernalia.

This letter is rapidly becoming a book, so will taxi over to the sack and sleep for a while. For who knows? Might just be an early morning briefing. So long . . .

Mar. 24th, '44

Howdy! Not much stuff to jabber about tonight. Mac and I are taking a five-day leave tomorrow if there isn't any mission. If there is one, we'll stick around and fly it and leave the next day. Guess we'll head for London. Had thought of going up to Edinborough (dunno how you spell that 'un) but the train service is so cockeyed quaint over here that neither of us relishes the thought of creeping about the island on one. The trip to London is just about all that we can stand for . . . (and I do mean stand). We'll lead a lazy life this leave . . . eat and sleep and see a show or two, have one drink apiece and tip our hats to all the working girls.

Couple of days ago finished off another of those missions which the papers call "American Bombers and Fighters Attacked Northern Germany Today in Poor Visibility." I kin think of better words than "poor" to describe that weather that day. Clouds started at 1,000 feet and were solid from there up to 38,000 feet. The mass of 'em stretched from Little America to Siberia and from Cheyenne to Inner Mongolia. And we wuz right smack in the middle of the whole mess trying to make rendezvous with our bombers somewhere over the Continent, all of us on instruments, etc.

Well, we get over the Continent and can't find any bombers. About that point, with 44 of us on instruments, we catch a lot of heavy flak that booms and thuds and breaks in black puffs all around us. Ships are twitching and jerking and pretty soon we dispatch a flight of four to feel its way up and up, to try to find the top of the overcast: and pretty soon some character hollers over the radio, "On top at 38,000, and I just seen Saint Pete swingin' them Pearly Gates open! Let's get the hell outta here!" Some other gent up ahead of me somewhere offers the clever, "Let's all Bail Out!" Wise cracks come from all angles after that one. About then, a voice from England tells us calmly that the bombers have aborted their mission and we might as well come back home. Then a voice from up ahead, the colonel's voice, comes out with a vulgar, "Curly, I'd rather eat turds for three hours than fly another one like this!" And Curly, the commander of another of our squadrons, comes right back with, "Well Joe, I got enuf right here in the cockpit to last you!" and about ten of us like to spin out, laughing. Boy, wuz we havin' fun! On the way homeward we let down thru the base of the overcast and I get flung off on a turn, get vertigo, and come a' roarin' out of the bottom of the stuff, almost on my back, and I catch a glimpse of a destroyer in the blacker color of overcast, and I think well the damn boat ain't in the sky, so I must be lookin' at water, and also I must be upside down. So I roll over and go home. That North Sea looked good for the first time. If all the sighs of relief could have been collected up, they would have filled all the barrage balloons in the ETO!!

All of us oddballs in C Flight now sport the Distinguished Flying Cross. Archy and Joe and Leo, Ed and Mac and I all got 'em in the General Orders on March 14.

Flown some 75 sorties now and feel quite the old hand at this racket . . . hi ho, nuthin' to it. Have learned plenty, thusly making each succeeding mission that much less hazardous, and our teamwork improves every time out. However, nothing ever happens twice in the same way here. We continue to change our tactics and Jerry continues to change his. We try to fox him and he tries to pull sundry whizzers on us. Verra interesting game, to say the least. Like a game of checkers . . . only in our case, the checkers go lickety-split, and when one of us jumps an opponent some Nazi insurance office gets itself some paperwork.

We sure like to fly behind Col. Richmond: couldn't have a better C.O. A fine pilot and cagey tactitian, and as we say, he looks after his boys! Remember one day we were back over England after a mission, and were plenty low on gas. So Gerst tells the Colonel that he has to land. The Colonel tells him to break away from the squadron and let down thru the overcast and "you ought to find a good field right below us . . . and be careful now, Joe." We got a kick out of that. Besides that, he leads us on all the tougher missions.

Opened the door the other night, and in walked a fine big Tomcat, a very handsome cat indeed. We treated him right and now we're stuck with him. But there may be some significance in the fact that, since he's been living with us, none of us has seen or heard a single, solitary mouse. We haven't fed the cat but he is fat and smiling all the time . . . could be! We name him "Turbo," for no good reason. Turbo has been a little shy of our company since Joe accidentally dropped the axe on his little head.

Soooo . . . will trundle off to the washroom and see if there's any hot water. If so, will soak for an hour and read an old Post.

Good night all, and will write again when I get back from this five-day leave . . . if I can, and I think I can . . .

Mar. 29, '44

Just back from five days in London. Mac and I had a swell time doing nothing. Saw a few shows, "Strike a New Note," for one, with Syd Fields making jokes.

The two boxes of food you sent were waiting for me when I got back. That seafood hit the spots that are missed by Spam and corned beef. We had a party, and et it all with glee and gusto.

Enclosed find picture of C-Flight. MacKean and Greene and me and Rocky sittin' on the wing: McKibben draped over the inboard guns, Parchesi-Joe Gerst, Heller, and Leo propping one another up on the ground.

This time in London, Mac and I made another feeble attempt at one of these here Cultural Tours we've been hearing about . . . flipped a bus and rode for ten minutes looking at the king's palace and the houses of Parliament and the Thames River, and at Hyde Park. Upon seeing the latter we got out of the bus and strolled thru the park listening to the screwballs orate from their soap-boxes, watching the swans swimming about in the lake, watching the crews raising several barrage balloons, watching the pretty gals flitting hither and yon, etc. Typical afternoon while on leave... and o yes, when it came time for the pubs to open up, we naturally were on hand to hoist a mug or two of bitters laced with gin.

Getting to be tomorrow already, so will take off. Note the lovely lady painted on the side of the Colonel's ship in the snapshot. Some dish, no?

Also heard from Tommy, who is still in the States but figgers to be leaving soon for parts unknown. Hope he comes over here . . .

Mar. 30, '44

Not much to orate about . . . just been discussing the flying abilities of birds with the lads. The main question before the house tonight is how the hell birds go up thru an overcast? They ain't got no instruments, so we figger they must fly strictly by the "seat of their pants" . . . only they ain't got no pants. We wonder if they often get vertigo and spin out . . . or if they tend to ice-up and do likewise? And how do they know which way the wind is blowing, as they always land properly upwind? Do they cock an eye down at the ground to see how many knots they're clocking and then figure to themselves that either they are or they ain't beating their wings fast enough to be going as fast they are? Wonder if they ever lose their tail feathers in a high speed dive? Do they ever get wing buffeting? Do they skid their turns and slip-in when they see they are about to overshoot a landing? Hmmmm? Do they remember landmarks when they are off on a cross-country flight or do they just stooge around on the way home til they locate their home base (nest to you, doc!) They ain't got maps like we have, and we never use 'em anyway. We use the stooge-around method of finding our way home. Birds ain't got nothin, tho. No zooop!

Anybody like fruit cake? We used to, but MacKean has received eleven of them in the mail in the last three months. He used to go with a wench who's old man runs a bakery. How about that?

This P-51 Mustang is quite a peashooter. Sure feels good to climb into that teeny little cockpit after roaming around in the old spacious Thunderbolt cockpit. Just barely have elbow room on either side, and a guy's got to squirm around to adjust various controls . . . little levers and dials and knobs stuck all about one . . . on the floor panels and under the seat and behind the seat and scattered about elsewhere.

MacKean is now cutting the latest fruit cake with a wicked looking Ghurka knife. We are choking down chunks of cake and making off-color remarks about his past. Turbo, our pet Tomcat, has taken a powder. Et all the mice in our hut and must have moved on to greener pastures. Boy, is this a hot letter. Weather lousy as usual. Nights chilly as usual. Hut full of wisecracks as usual. Everybody's happy, as usual.

April 3, '44

Allo, Yank . . . Midnight in the ETO, and it ain't a fit night out fer man nor beast. The rain is rattling down on our tin roof and dripping thru various cracks and holes onto the floor . . . our stove is turning out a lot of heat, tho, and it is really quite clubby in here. Now and then a wee mouse scampers across the floor bound on some nefarious bit of business or other. (Since Turbo-the-cat left us, the mice have moved back into the old stand!) I do believe that Spring has moved our way; the days have been warmer and we don't have to climb thru quite so much cloud-cover in order to find some sunshine. Also, bits of poetry flit thru my mind, to wit:

"'Twas an early day in Spring,
All de boids wuz on de wing.
My woid! How absoid!
I thot de wings wuz on de boid!"

Spent the day puttering around my newest ship; painted up spots where the camouflage had worn off (might have been dragging her pore fuselage thru treetops at 300-plus mph!) Painted some fancy blue paint all over her nose and had the squadron painter do a mighty fancy job on the name and insignia. She looks plenty hot now: the name of my ship is now "The Joker" and is written on the left side of her long and pointed nose, just below the exhaust stacks. Red letters trimmed with yellow edging. Worked up a dandy joker to paint on for the insignia: a grinning skull with a jester's hat perched thereon. If I can't shoot 'em down, I'll scare 'em to death! The crew is sanding and waxing the rest of the ship and she's sure getting a sleek look. Quite a hunk of machinery.

The boys are now involved in a bitter and profane discussion of high-blowers and low-blowers, props and English spark plugs, pitch and torque and guns and armor and stoppages and so forth and so on around and around. Woops . . . just got sidetracked over to Archy's tru love, who lives either in St. Louis or Milwaukee—he can't remember which. And now they're hashing over our various ancestries: Rocky sez he's half Norwegian and half American Indian. Claims that 1,000 years ago when Lief the Lucky got up to Minneapolis, that's how it happened. McKibben claims Scotch-Irish and Gerst sez he dunno. Pennsy Dutch, he guesses. Wot a performance.

Ted with the Joker, his beloved—and short-lived—Mustang at Bodney Airfield.

Now the talk turns to New York City. We just heard about three Navy pilots who buzzed the Empire State Building and got tossed into the brig for their troubles. Hell, we worked it over one day good and proper and didn't get caught. Archy wants to tour down Broadway in his '51 at 500 mph and terrify everybody.

Hear old Russ Craig got his tracks down in Italy someplace. (Made Captain, to you. Two shiny bars—railroad tracks—hence the slang to cover the situation.) Tex writes from India saying he's due for leave in the States pretty soon. As for me, I'll be there when I get there. So, love & kisses . . .

P.S . . . "An amoeba named Joe and his brother
Were out drinking a toast to each other.
In the midst of their quaffing,
They split their sides laffing,
And discovered that each was a mother."

April 9, '44

So you ain't heard from me in three weeks, eh? Well, I know I write about once a week and when I get eager I shoot off a couple a week. So quit nibbling your fingernails and relax. You'll probably get three or four in a bunch.

This is Easter Sunday, and what a shock when we walk into the mess hall for breakfast. Tablecloths on the tables and daffydills in vases and everything quite fancy, including the rare dish of two (2) real hen-type eggs. Real live eggs with yolks, and fried sunnyside up. Some feed. The weather was pretty punk today, but the group flew out on a good hot mission, a freelance sort of hunt. The Chaplain even came to briefing and gave us a little talk, a quick prayer, wished us luck, and sent up another flare or two. And then we go out and massacree some more Nazzys. Low-level stuff, and we shoot up a bunch of trains, flak-towers, grounded air-craft, soldats, etc. We had a good day of it.

There was an Easter service up by the control tower this a.m., too, right alongside the C-Flight dispersal area(!) Three Mustangs were parked to form a background and the chaplain spoke from the wing of one of 'em . . . more daffydills scattered about on the ship's noses, and the ground crews used rows of belly-tanks for seats. Two-thirds of the pilots took refuge in our hut where we sat and drank ale and pondered the devious ways of life. Quite a different setting than that of the service you folks attended, no doubt.

MacKean is now a captain, good fer him! Also some more names for C-Flight aircraft: Gerst's ship is "Brom Baby," Mac's is "Miss Lace" (after that slinky wench in Milt Caniff's strip). And Greene's is "Geronimo" on account of becuz we fondly call Frank that because he has the big hooked nose like the Indian.

Have three movies per week here on the field. Take 'em all in, and wot a variety. Last week even get Sinatra in a few reels of corn. The boys fail to go for Franky. Druther see Hells Angels or some such white-man's movie. But the movies we like best to see are the ones we make ourselves . . . every time we fire our guns we get a movie of the target. Makes for very interesting stuff.

I read in an English paper that March was the driest month in 27 years. Great balls of fire!! People must wear hip boots around here in normal times: I am surprised that Englishmen still have lungs instead of gills. Evolution will probably fix that up for them during the next million years.

We have also found a sure way to tell when we cross from Germany into Holland or Belgium, when we come heading for home on the deck (at zero altitude). When the peasants quit throwing rocks at us and begin waving, then we've crossed the border. Lot of truth in that, too. Most of the Dutch, Belgians, and French people wave to us, altho some of 'em run like a son of a gun. Collaborators, no doubt.

All to gab about today, so will fold up shop and drift over to the bar, for supper.

April 14, '44

Things have been booming in this neck of the woods lately, and our boy Cutler has been having a great time of it (note clippings). You ought to've heard him whoopin' and hollerin' over the radio when he got his finger blowed off! His radio was shot up so that he was transmitting without re- alizing it (or caring), and the air was full of lively commentary ensuing from his cockpit: "@!–#!!!&!@" and then he'd fly up alongside one of the boys and wave his stump gaily at 'em, and follow it up with choice com- ments relating to the dirty illegitimate Hun who'd done it. Well, Frank flew all the way from deep within Germany to England a-bleedin' like a fountain and flyin' with the stick between his knees, and then shot a perfect landing at a RAF coastal airdrome. A good fighter pilot, that gent.

Flew non-operational today...just playing around amongst the clouds. Nice puffy white ones for a change. Also got my hand in on some fancy stuff with the new ship. Wrung 'er out as a good ship ought to be wrung out and enjoyed the couple of hours more than I've enjoyed anything for a long time. Ratted around with a Spit and whipped him technically along with a couple of P-38s I caught stooging along. This was theoretically a test-flight, as I got a new vertical fin on my ship, the old one having col- lected up some flak that rendered it rather unserviceable.

Dunno, but I wouldn't be surprised if a lot of us guys apply for exten- sions on our tours of duty over here: We figger we can't win the war sittin' on our fannies back in the States. Besides that, right now we're making single-engine fighter history, and we hate to miss out on any of the fun. A couple of years ago aviation experts would have declared impossible the things we're doing right now with our peashooters!

With the weather so mild of late, we've been taking long strolls thru the country in the evenings. C-Flight goes out en masse—Nature lovers one and all. Shooting bullfrogs with our .45s, throwing rocks at rabbits and pheasants, trying to spear fishes in the crick with pointed sticks, etc. We found a porcupine crawling along the other evening and looked him over. Won't be long until the daylight hours stretch from seven a.m. til midnight (and then we'll be doing plain and fancy flying . . .)

I'll be having a lot of fun from now on, over here, and will be able to tell you less and less in letters, as censorship will undoubtedly become more strict as the invasion date comes nearer.

April 16, '44

A gay time of it in this neck of the woods—a bit on the destructive side! At last have squared things with the taxpayers for all the ships I've cracked up at one time or another. Been flying with Woodrow Anderson, a dyed-in-the-wool Texan (if I can mention wool and Texas in the same breath.) This gent is a fine friend and a reckless guy in the cockpit, and we have much sport whenever we end up coming home together. Railroad time-tables in the Reich are sure in one helluva mess . . .

I swore by the old Thunderbolt, but doggoned if this Mustang doesn't put her to shame. I kin do anything my bloodthirsty little heart desires with this baby. And scenes of violent action have been ours these days, ho ho ho! Someday I hope to orate about such stuff to you . . . a three-ring circus and a barrel of monkeys all together, plus the all too obvious knowledge that folks on the ground are mighty mad at us, and show their objections in tremendous barrages of flak, some of which is a mite too accurate. Oddest of all is the sight of great showers of light machine-gun fire. Some of those Huns couldn't hit a bull in the stern with a shotgun. But brother, we sure put on an air show when Jerry cuts loose with his heavy flak: nasty jet-black and jagged puffs suddenly will appear in quantity off the wingtip. I dodge and it follows . . . I swoop and it swoops . . . I swerve and it swerves . . . I zig when I should have zagged and then I can hear the stuff going wham wham wham wham, and when I hear that I go hog-wild, fill the cockpit with many controls and put on a show that would take first prize at any exhibition of aerobatics. The heavy stuff throws up these sooty explosions, big as a barn . . . the medium stuff makes brownish puffs the size of a couple of washtubs, and we don't pay much attention to that. The very light low-level stuff is often tracer, and that is very spectacular to see. They arc up past you, and all you gotta do is to kick rudder and leave it off to one side.

That heavy flak climbs skyward at roughly a thousand feet per second, so if flying at twenty-thousand feet and you peer downward and spot the flash of gun-muzzles blasting, you just count to fifteen or so and make a turn, and in five seconds you will note a quartet of black puffs appear right where you should have been. But inasmuch as we don't often look ground-ward, we automatically change course every few seconds, to foul up Jerry's tracking devices.

Flying low over Germany (anywhere from five to five hundred feet) you can see at any given time six or eight hidden gun muzzles blinking and winking your way. Just light machine-gun fire, and we don't bother over that, except now and then to extinguish one with a short squirt.

We don't often worry, and we also hope that our folks don't fret too much over us. This ain't no marble game and people sometimes get hurt, but none of the pilots in this crew ever figgers he'll catch a packet of lead. And you know me!! I've got more luck that Carter has little liver pills. (And outside of the luck factor, I kin outfly any character who ever clumb into a peashooter—confidentially!) Most of us are getting good and mad now, and when we fly these days we see red from start to finish.

My crew chief, German, got busted the other day for a slight case of AWOL, and since then he's worked twice as hard on my ship. Wants his stripes back and I'll get 'em for him. The ship shows his efforts, too . . . runs like a Swiss watch, only faster. This German is a type, allright. Best durned mechanic on the line and can diagnose the slightest aches and pains of my engine by just running 'er up and listenin' to her tick with his home-made stethoscope (he sticks one end of a screwdriver into his ear and places the other end here and there on the machinery . . .) I told him today when I landed that the engine today was worth approximately seventy-five billion dollars, cash money!

Sent you a DFC today and hope you get it o.k. I often think of home and outside of the fact that I'm kind of enjoying this racket, I also know the whys and wherefores and I do know what we're fighting for. Tell you all about it someday . . . ho ho ho!

Had a few beers tonight at the Club and walked from there into A-Flight's hut. Had only been there a short while when I saw a duck waddle across the floor. From under one bunk, across the floor, and under another bunk. I looked around, careful-like, but nobody else seemed to notice this phenomenon. So I kept my mouth shut and shrugged it off as just another symptom of flak-happiness. Just before I left, however, I poked my head back thru the doorway and casually asked if they kept a duck in their hut. They said yes, Thank God.

April 18, '44

Letter from Tommy Price yesterday. He's over here with me now, and only about 150 miles away, so first chance I get will fly down and say hello. Sure be good to see that monkey again.

Love the new ship. Comparison between that eight-gunned, barrel-chested bull I used to operate around in and this fast, slim little fighter is about the same as the difference between working with a cutlass and a rapier.

Note the enclosed clipping . . . tell you what dandy varieties of mischief has been cooking over here.

Weather has fouled up again and we're sitting around waiting for it to break so we can go out again. Also hoping that it does clear up before they do send us out. None of us really enjoy driving about thru fog and heavy cloud at our rapid pace! Non-habit forming, to say the least.

Another learned discussion arose tonight as to whether birds fly inside of clouds. They ain't got no instruments at all. We aim to catch a pigeon and put some tape over his eyes and then stick him in the butt with a needle, and carefully observe his blind takeoff. The odds right now are five-to-one that he spins in. Science is a wonderful thing!

No other news, just a short one to keep the postman happy . . .

Chapter 14

* *

Spring Preparations

April 23, '44

By all rights I ought to be buzzing around over the old country right at this point, but blew a tire while taxiing out for takeoff, so am rotting away here on the ground. Doggone the luck anyway. Am going on 48-hour leave tomorrow and will go down to pay a small visit to my ornry cousin Tom Price and his Thunderbolt. Will return a full report to his paw, as I imagine he'd like to know the TRUTH. Tom sez he'd bring me a jug of good stuff from the States, so aim now to collect.

Ol' McKibben blasted one the other day. Boy, have we been havin' fun these days. Really a lovely business, this. The weather is going our way for a change, and promises to stay pretty fair. But still, now and then, we go up into bleak cloudy stuff. Any one of us would rather fly up and down over Happy Valley all day long than mix it up with old man weather. By the way, Happy Valley is an infamous stretch of hostile territory running for miles up the Ruhr Valley. Absolutely lousy with accurate, heavy flak. Common knowledge in flying circles over here. We generally avoid it, but sometimes run afoul of it when "navigating" over a heavy overcast. I came home alone the other day from Berlin, on instruments all the way. Pore ol' carburetor liked to give out on me. I calculate finally that I've made land-fall-out and am now over the North Sea. So I quit zig-zagging and head straight for home. I fly straight and level at fifteen thousand feet for five minutes. I light up a smoke. And BLONK BLOCK BLONK! Some Jerry down below has been rubbing his hands together and waiting for the right moment to pull the trigger on me. He does, and four jet-black bursts appear some three-quarters of an inch off my right wingtip. Then a red burst. I black myself out taking violent, instinctive evasive action, lose my cigarette, oxygen mask, etc. So I zig-zag for a while, and all the while pondering my navigational abilities. I steer more northward for a while, then let down thru the soup to find nothing but a great disk of shimmering water beneath me. My radio is busted somewhat, and when I finally do contact England for a "fix," I find myself to be halfway to Norway. I limp home on half an engine and land hours after I theoretically should have run out of fuel. Live & learn, I allus say.

Note in today's *Stars & Stripes* where a Mustang crashed in Sweden. Another fine navigator!

Me and my crew are really thicker'n flies. Nacherly, I hate to have any other pilot fly my ship, as there are some knuckleheads in the outfit—guys who habitually substitute brawn for brains, and are mighty rough on a precision machine like this ship. So whenever I land and taxi back to my revetment, I announce officially that something's haywire with the ship, whereupon Sgt. German rips a couple of panels off'n the cowling to make it look good. So far, no one but me has flown er, and she's the best ship on the line. I've had a couple of very fine airplanes ruined by mishandling on the part of some meat-headed numbskulls.

Your letters have been arriving at various odd intervals, and generally not in order, which makes for interesting reading. In one there might be a squawk about not hearing from me for a month, and in the next you'll be all hopped up on account of you just got six letters from Merrie Olde. Also at weekly intervals I get an apologetic note from sundry olde gals, telling me how they got hitched to some character. Boy, am I going to have to stage a roundup when I git back in the States again. A new assortment. Hell's Belles!

Such a wonderful evening, warm sunny and bright, that guess I'll have me a brew or two and prowl into the local village.

Big two-day leave tomorrow, and will write again when I get back to this neck of the woods.

April 25, '44

The pace is stepped up these days. But the actual invasion, when it occurs, won't make much difference to this gang for we've been fighting at close quarters with the enemy all along. Another series of encounters won't make much difference to us, for we've been facing the most vicious opposition Jerry can offer. Despite some bitter flak met when carrying out some recent attacks, Lady Luck keeps "the Joker" zigging when she ought to zig and zagging when she ought to zag.

This game has its interesting moments. We strafed an airdrome not long ago with unforeseen developments occurring in the process. Sixteen of us with eight ships coming in at treetop level and eight others navigating the low flights in to the target by remote control. So the top eight, including your correspondent, are to act as guinea pigs, drawing anti-aircraft fire away from the low-level attackers. We are to arrive over the airdrome in question a few seconds before the low ships scoot in to deliver their strafing. That at least is the plan. But we arrive over the airdrome as planned and do some fancy flying, teasing the gun batteries into action. So they concentrate on us with a terrific barrage and we dance around like fools with the stuff pounding all around us, and we're only at two thousand feet. But the low ships don't show up on schedule, for they have met seven Jerry fighters who've just taken off and are involved in a dogfight in amongst the treetops. We know nothing of this, however, and continue to draw flak until driven away by the sheer weight of it. The boys at low level do a good job, knocking down five '190s, and then they go in to strafe, meeting concentrated flak in the process.

We got a new C.O. now. Enclosed find candid shot of Willie O. Jackson who leads the bunch these days. Sure like this gent . . . a real friend, one of the bunch and has earned our respect and admiration both at the bar and in the air. Generally got a big twinkle in his eye, Willie O.

April 30, '44

Been quite a spell since I last wrote, but have been keeping pretty busy these days. Have had a particularly fine week of it: flown enuf to keep me happy and have seen a lot of country I never thought I'd see from the cockpit of a little fighter plane. Been milling thru the thin air from the Baltic to Lake Constance, and all the territory in between. Most delightful scenery, now that Spring has come to Europe.

Southern France is perfectly dandy with its rolling farmlands and great patches of green forest and its many winding rivers. When I fly over there, I often think of all the ancient stories I've read of the going's-on there in the old days. Thought the other day that one of those old armor-plated knights would have had to spend his lifetime clattering madly at a gallop in order to see the country that I viewed in a few short hours. And I saw the country as a whole and not as individual trees and hills and river crossings, as did he. Paris is a pretty sight, the way it's laid out, with the Seine sweeping thru the middle of town in great bends . . . could see the Eiffel Tower and various other odds and ends about town.

Engine conked out over Germany the other day, but I got her kicking and headed for home and just made the coast. Set the Joker down dead-stick on a coastal bomber 'drome. Mac escorted me home and two or three times radioed for Air Sea Rescue when I thought I was going to have to bail out into the North Sea. And I just limp over the coast when, with a loud bang and puff of black smoke, the engine quits for good. So I barrel downhill and breeze into a new field, with long concrete runway placed beneath me by Lady Luck. Too late I see it is under construction, and as I try to set her down intact I see great quantities of dark-complected folks fleeing for their lives on either side like black snow curling out from in front of a V-snowplow. But nobody gets hurt and I have just enuf speed left at the end of the runway to roll off onto a taxi-strip and spin 'er around neatly in a revetment. So I sit on the wing wiping sweat from my brow and taking a long hard swig from my flask, and this ground-Colonel roars up on a motorcycle. "Gawdammit!" he cries, "Whatcha mean landing on a new runway. Who gave ya permission to land here?" Well I sez, "Jeez, I'm even glad to see you, Mac. Here, have a drink!" And I adds that the Laws of Gravity gave me permission to land here. So in three or four hours my own crew shows up in a jeep. German fixes the carburetor, which he finds to have filings in it as tho by sabotage. So I rev 'er up and fly home.

Have forsaken all my faithful correspondents of late . . . been so preoccupied with the business at hand that people who aren't right here seem to be a million miles away in another world entirely. Am generally so bushed at night that I just wet my whistle and then hit the hay. Eat irregularly as usual and snooze five or six hours a night and spend the better part of each day either in or around my ship. Pretty good life.

Listened tonight to "Calais One, Bremen and Cologne!" a popular Nazi program we all enjoy. They get off with some comical news broadcasts about what we didn't do over there lately. Tonight they put on a corny request program, with a regular old fashioned weiner-schnitzel band to play the music—tuba and horns and an accordion and some gent with a raucous whiskey voice to do the vocals. Got more laughs outta that music than we've had for the past ten days, which is a few. One of the lads, Frascotti by name, rolls up his pants cuffs and turns up his blouse collar and comes in sporting a bow tie and big handkerchief in his breast pocket. Quite a character, and if the taxpayers could have seen it they'd have folded up. I'm tellin' you, you could swap any twenty pilots in this outfit for any twenty inmates of any hi-class booby-hatch and no one could tell the difference in either institution. Like to have a recording of radio chatter during an encounter with the Jerries: guys cussin' and hollerin' back and forth in shrill admiration of the destruction going all around them. "Hey Mac, lookit that great big fire I started, willya!"

"Didja see that bassard hit the ground!!" "Hey sport, you're catching some flak from that tower across the field . . . wait a minnit and I'll get that S.O.B!" Stuff like that pours thru the earphones and makes most enjoyable listening.

Didn't quite make it over to see Tommy yet, but hope to soon. Len ought to be showing up over here pretty soon, too. A lot of his B-24 tribe in the area.

Weather fine of late, and a relief from the flying in the fog of last winter. Much easier on the noives. Sunshine is really wonderful stuff. Wonderful.

Can't figger out where this year has disappeared to. April has just plain vanished. Just about payday again. Lucky couple of poker games has ended me up with a pocketful of green. Most unusual . . .

Couple of Texans in the outfit, Woodrow Wilson Anderson and W. Brashean, both I think part Injun and plenty hot pilots. Wild men indeed. Wonderful bunch of characters in this outfit. None like 'em left in the States, for the whole tribe of people like these is flying somewhere in this war. Shiftless lot of vagabonds . . .

A sweet ship, this Mustang. Could drive this baby right thru the subway in Chicago at 500 mph without twitching a whisker. Ever I git a chance to work that town over with a fighter, it'll get the peachiest buzz job ever seen in the USA.

Big discussion now arising in the hut. Discussion is too polite a word for it. Knives will be flashing soon: within five minutes at the rate the argument is developing. I'd better quit this letter and join in . . .

May 1, '44

Things bin pickin' up a bit of late. Am so pooped out by nightfall that I don't feel like writing many letters. They get us out of bed at the weirdest hours nowadays. Beats the hell out of lying around doing nothing, as was the case last winter. Some of us are almost getting to look healthy.

Another squadron party last Saturday night. Everybody had a peachy time. The doc brewed us up some more of that kickapoo joy-juice of his. This party was most enjoyable and all that happened to me this time was inexplicable loss of two buttons off my dress blouse and the fadeout of a row of service ribbons from same. And the next morn, bright and early —too early to be bright, for the sun had not yet come up—we climb into our ships and operate around the Reich. What a story! Captain Andrew really did some gory work and the simple word "hamburger" will always refresh my memory. Andy is quite a gent. The most precise and deliberate

Ted describes Capt. Stephen Andrews: "One-a-Day Andrew was forced down on a shuttle raid en route to Russian. Turned up a P.W. in the same camp as Col. Richmond. Andy was mild-mannered and non-alcoholic on the ground, a perfect gentleman. In the air he was the most precise, calculating, cool, and fearless fighter pilot the Jerries ever met, and after a victory he would analyze his kill with complete sangfroid."

pilot in the squadron. Cool like the cucumber and very analytical: most curious guy I ever knew, he likes details and inquires in his mild voice about every little encounter he hears about. For instance, should I tell Andy that I'd just killed a rabbit with a rock, he might ask: (1) Just where did you first see this rabbit, Ted? (2) Was he hopping, running, walking, or sitting? (3) How big a rock did you throw and what shape was it? (4) Did the rabbit see you? (5) How fast was he going and what deflection did you allow and how much did you lead him? (6) Was the rabbit killed instantly or did you have to throw a second rock? (7) Did you examine the body to see why the rock killed him? Etc.

You can figure out what happens to any enemy ship Andy meets up with. He gets one a day. He came back home mad the other day, saying he'd gotten too close to this '109 when he'd pulled the trigger. The enemy plane sprayed oil all over the captain's ship, thus blinding him. He was unable to shoot at the second Jerry ship and that's why he was sore. Hates to let one get away. Next, he sez, he will shoot from a greater angle so as to let the oil spray miss his own ship. Andrew is a very quiet, mild-mannered guy on the ground; and a perfect officer and gent indeed. But in an airplane the guy goes nuts, complete.

The mornings we fly early, we are all well party-fied. Indeed, some quit playing with the ladies in favor of strapping on a 'chute. So we all close one eye on takeoff, give 'em the throttle and away we go, higher'n kites. Well, four of us forget to open up our formation when we cross the enemy coast, with the result that we all get flak-holes. Willie O. Jackson's canopy falls off over Paris and he is quite cold, for we are up at 25,000 feet. So he heads for home, taking his flight with him, me included. We land and continue the party while the rest of the squadron bores on inland. So this Andrew character spots a Focke-Wulf 190, gets on his tail, and starts shooting. Can't hit the damn thing, so he closes up fast, overshoots and flies tight formation with this Jerry fighter. Andy waves at the other pilot, drops back, and starts shooting again, this time with accuracy. The Jerry pilot bails out and is swept back squarely into Andy's propeller. Splat. Usually a blow of such intensity would knock down a fighter plane, but this Jerry hits squarely in the hub, with an equal strain on all parts of the propeller. Well, pal Archy is flying alongside, sightseeing, and inasmuch as this is a gory sight and Arch's stomach is full of party-type butterflies, he pulls off one fur flying boot and upchucks into it and tosses the works overboard. On the way home, then, when over the Channel, Archy figures that one boot is no damn good, so he tosses the other out and down into the briny deep. Andrew gets his ship home intact, lands, crawls out of the cockpit, walks to the propeller, picks a scrap of flying suit from a bolt and pockets it. "Good souvenir," he sez, and walks away.

I gotta fold up for the night, so will end this tender letter and say good-nite to all . . .

May 6, '44

Long time no write to you, Toots, but today get your letter and find within two postcards. One of an ancient building and one of an outlaw stretched out on a slab. Got a good laff. You have your moments, don't you? Heh heh heh (hysterics). My crew chief got to painting on my aircraft today. New result wuz that you now have one fifty-caliber machine-gun named after you. "Toots" it sez in white letters over the muzzle on the leading edge of the wing. My crew chief named the starboard Dot & Millie. Wife and kiddy, perhaps, or maybe it's a couple of dames he knows in Hartford. I dunno.

I spoke too soon about the weather. It wuz nice while it lasted but then it double-crossed us. Last night it rained, hailed, etc. The moon would come out and then a hailstone would hit you in the eye as you looked up to check the weather. Today I awoke feeling fit as a slightly worn fiddle. I peer out the door at the sky. Blue! I hollers at the boys . . . ought to have a mission this morning! By the time I put my duds on and head for the mess hall, the sky is cluttered up with stuff. By the time I finish eating, it is raining. Then the sun comes out and shows a peachy rainbow. Then it rains. All day, the same. I win ten pounds playing poker down at the pilots' hut. I lose eleven pounds tonight playing poker in the Club. I stick three pounds in the slot machine in the Club and all I get is a sore thumb from cranking the cockeyed machine. I go to take a bath, but run out of warm water halfway thru and end up shivering at the bar with a rum & coke to keep me warm. I run for the hut to beat McKibben and Rauk out of the typewriter, and here I am! Typical bad-weather day.

Good-weather day, fly five or eight hours and so pooped out that I hit the hay early and wake up tired. Seen a bunch of swell scenery lately . . . most everything from icebergs to alps.

One of my minor pleasures is to paint my external drop-tanks with all kinds of insulting data addressed to the good folk of the Reich. Then when they're empty, I look all over for some city to dive bomb with 'em. "Plunk" they go into squarehead's backyard. Ho ho.

Enjoying life these days? Understand that meat rationing is tightened a bit. Buy up all the Spam you can corner and put it on the Rock Island tracks and sit and watch the trains mash it. Boy would that be fun! Getting two gallons a week? Hmmm. I use that much checking my magnetos (or dry-cleaning my blouse), I think. Good ol' petrol.

I kin understand Limey, now. Walk into a local jernt and the innkeeper sez: "'Elloo, Yenk! Uttleitbee?" I say, "Pint o' arf anarf, if you ain't gotny spirits, ol' cock." Then he sez, "Attlebee nyepencehaypenny, chum." Stuff like that there. Limey flying talk is quite quaint. "'Twas a wizard prang, chum . . . I finked the kite and clobbered the bloke. Rawther a good show, wot?" Translated which means: "Was a damn good rat-race, pal. I maneuvered my ship into position and shot him down. Pretty interesting deal, ain't it?" See? It ain't hard to savvy.

Enuf of this idle chatter. McKibben is hanging over the typewriter... he must write his nightly letter to his beloved 'Nita, which gal he aims to marry up with when he gets his 30-day leave. Speaking of 30-day leaves, they are purely figments of the imagination at present. So don't expect to see my ugly mug until you see it. I'm having a pretty good time over here anyway. Hi ho. So long for a while . . .

May 10, '44

Just back from a 48-hour leave. Paid ol' Tom Price a visit! He's many hours away from here by train, but it was sure worthwhile to see him. Haven't laughed so hard and long for full many a moon. He's in the best of good health (not anymore) and as full of baloney as ever. He's just started combat flying and is having a lot of fun. He's living in a tent on a makeshift airdrome, but is not far from a good-sized town.

I located him about one in the afternoon, and when I called him on his promise to fetch me some good booze, he hauled out a jug of rotgut rum, explaining he'd drunk the good stuff already. So we scampered into town for the afternoon and evening, hashing over old times en route and having many a hearty laugh over the strange sight of the two of us strolling up and down the streets of an English city. Tom naturally knows all the best people in the local black markets, and we had a fine dinner of bacon and fresh eggs and hot rolls. All this rationed food he accomplished by a hot line of flattery paid to the elderly and fat proprietress of a dinky little restaurant. He sez, "Teddy me boy, that ol' gal will do anything for me . . . watch!" and he calls her over to the table and whispers in her ear a bit. The old dame laughs and sez, "Tommy . . . I've lived right here for fifty years now and if you want a bottle of Scotch, I know where I can get it for you!" Scotch is next to impossible to get hold of, but it looks like ol' Tom is set for the duration.

Well, seeing as the pubs were closed at that time of day, we went to a little old movie house and sat up in the balcony swapping lies for a couple of hours. When we emerged the rum was all gone, Tom had the usherette

Tom Price, a first cousin and one of Ted's best childhood friends, ended up at a nearby base flying fighters. Ted's sister Caroline says that the cousins were "two of a kind—if that's possible."

lined up for future reference, and neither of us was feeling much pain. We carried on from there, making the rounds of the pubs, drinking our brew, and whoopin' and hollerin' like a couple of monkeys. At three a.m. it was raining hard and cold and I crawled aboard the slow train to London, leaving Tom to his own problem, that of getting back to his base. I imagine he didn't make it. We're gonna get together later on this month. What a character!

Got a letter from Len and will pay him a visit very soon. He's stationed very nearby. Wish I'd known that earlier, but will round him up first chance I have. Be good to see Len. He tells me that ol' pal Russ Craig is in a doubtful category. May be a rumor, but he'll turn up in the wash somewhere. Sure good to start seeing old friends over here with me. Makes it seem one big happy family. Sure wish Tom could be in this outfit with me. There'd be hell to pay if the two of us were operating together. Hot dawg!

My favorite aircraft the Joker is now playing submarine due to an incident occurring while I was on leave. Remember I told you of that bad carburetor . . . flew home from Berlin on the primer alone (technical rep. from the factory still says it can't be done!). Well, that liked to've torn the engine outta the mounts, she ran so rough. So I put in for a new ship, knowing that the structure of the fuselage was badly strained. So some guy doesn't think so and takes the ship out dive bombing, and she shed the wings and goes into the target with bombs, pilot, and all. Sweating out a new ship now.

Fine weather now and London looked pretty nice for a change. Spring has resulted in a lot of people floating around. Met a rare character in a shop . . . the old gent runs a little silver shop on New Bond Street and I dropped in to buy a little flask I see in the window. So the ol' duffer fills me full of malarkey about flying DH-4s back in the first war, and we go into his office for a scotch-and-soda to hash things over. Regular ol' Kentucky Colonel type.

May 12, '44

Another day and perfect weather. Flew today for the first time in four or five days, and it felt pretty good to get back in the thick of things. When in London on the last two-day's leave, the outfit went out and intercepted 150 single-engine German fighters who were about to attack a flock of bombers. We got 35 victories, aerial combat, of which 27 were destroyed. Big dogfight. We lost one ship . . . which goes to prove something.

Spent yesterday afternoon and evening with Len. Where do you suppose the guy is stationed? About four miles from our little fighter base! So I grab me a bicycle and pedal lickety-split over hill and dale and locate his airdrome. I inquire around a bit and find out he lives in hut no. 32. I bust in there and ask one of the boys where he is, and I find Len ol' boy parked in front of a washtub in the shower room, industriously washing his sox. We shoot the breeze merrily for a while and he gives me some goodies and I give him a swig out of the wee flask I brought along for the purpose, and we retire to the club nearby, hash things over and drink a stein or two of English brew. So he gets a bicycle and we peddle to town, where we purchase a jug of scotch from a peddler. We get home later.

He looks fine, and despite his groaning he likes his job. He's just starting into business over here, and our gang escorted his outfit today. Soon as he gets some freedom, the two of us will be able to get together often as we like. Slick deal, the two of us being only a couple miles apart. He's flying the best ship in its class and will be finished with his tour in no time at all . . . doesn't take those bomber boys long to build up their flying hours.

Len Telfer, Ted's best friend in Chicago from kindergarten on through high school, who ended up at an airfield a few miles from Bodney flying B-24s. He was killed in action in the summer of 1944 on the same day Ted went MIA in France.

Bet the house and yard look pretty at this time of year: spend a lot of time puttering about, poking at various plants and casting a weather eye at the lawn, etc. I do a lot of walking between the hut and flight line, daily. I walk over one particular field every day. A few months ago it was sod, then I walked over it after it was plowed, then seeded (with a thousand seagulls eating the seed out of the furrows), then I tramped over the sprouts, and daily thereafter I noticed how fast the stuff was coming up. Now the stuff is six inches high. Hope I don't have to pick my way thru the shocks of grain!

All for tonight, as sad cries are being raised about the noise this thing makes. It's not a noiseless typewriter by any stretch of the imagination.

Got a new ship now, a silver one, and the crew is working hard to get 'er in shape for combat. Ready purty soon. Don't like flying different ships every day, and they're all different in minor ways. Temperamental little gals, they are, and they'll snap at you if you don't treat 'em right . . .

May 16, '44

Howdy: sitting here in the pilot's hut with time on my hands. A few of us gotta stand by during the night and tonight it falls to Frank and Mac and me. The rain outside is driving down hard on the tin roof, as it's done now for several days without much letup. Greene is collapsed in an easy chair by the fireplace sucking on a tall bottle of beer. McKibben does likewise. Our four mechanics are boredly wandering about, wishing they were elsewhere. I'm a-sittin close to the fire writing this peachy letter.

The squadron area is a sea of mud, but we needed it badly. The field was getting pretty dusty and all our recent flying has worn a lot of grass off the runway. Mebbe this rainy spell will give it a chance to come back.

Did get a chance to put my new ship thru her paces. Took her up for a couple of hours and ratted all over the sky, wrung her out and twisted her tail seven ways from Sunday, and finished off with a long vertical power dive during the course of which I build up a censored number of them good mph's. Then went out over the sea and checked my guns, firing at a sandbar. Then shagged a Mosquito (RAF) across the deck with everything up to the firewall (full throttle to you) . . . then made a couple of strafing passes at a bunch of Limey soldiers I found in a chow line at their camp. They all ran like a bunch of sheep. Hope someday I catch a like number of Jerry soldiers flatfooted like that. Pestered a bunch of bombers

for a while, making dry runs on them just for fun. O, I had a fine couple
of hours, just sat there in that little cockpit and stooged all over the sky
having fun. Like to fly alone like that: flying with a gang of other ships
gets kind of old.

Ain't figgered a new name for the ship. The last ship I named the Joker,
but she turned out to be a practical joker indeed. Liked to've put in the
drink of couple of times . . . ho ho. Now I got a new gal, right off the
production line, and she's got a couple of added features as to performance.

Len returned the visit I paid him a while back. The other day he and
two of his pals came a-pedaling over to see me via the back roads. We had
a beer or two or three and passed the time of day and then I showed them
my ship. They nacherly turn quite green with envy. One thing I gotta say
for them truck drivers . . . they do know a good ship when they see one.
Altho I am surprised that they can still recognize an airplane after all their
experience at operating around the sky with one of those clunks of theirs.
Len and I had supper together here and spent a short, enjoyable evening
in the Club. Swapped lies and had a few scotch-and-sodas and became
involved in a small game of showdown poker, at a pound a throw. At
which game Len and I each walk off with thirty or forty bucks of somebody's dough. He had to get back early, so I hire him a jeep from the motor
pool and we load his bike on behind and away he goes. Those bomber
boys have a sad life. They have to get to bed about eight o'clock in the
evening, for they are more often than not awakened at the sly hour of one
or two a.m. for their briefing sessions. Whereas we gents can get away with
sleeping until two minutes before start-engine time. Ah-ha!

While over at Len's bomber base I notice what a different type of pilot
drives those bombers. Nice quiet lot of well-dressed officers and gentlemen! Over here in my outfit, a rowdy crew of profane jerks wearing assorted costumes that'd do credit to a band of gypsies. Of course, it might
be that we've been over here long enuf to go to seed, too.

Due to a recent communiqué from the Supreme Command (the big
wheels who run this fighter command), I won't be home as soon as I
thought I might be home. Gimme another three or four months and I
could possibly be showing my face around them parts for a month or so.
Anyway, after sweating out the puny preliminary bouts, I hate to think of
missing the main event. Won't be too long before I'll be celebrating an

anniversary: A year in this dismal swamp. Ho ho ho. Who'd a thunk it? Anybody told me I'd spend a year living in an overgrown section of corrugated iron pipe in the middle of the rain-swept moors of England, I would'a spit in his eye. Anybody ever tells me I might do it again, I will. (Will probably spend another year at it, that is, if some general tells me I will!)

Flash . . . ! Moved out of one Nissen hut into another Nissen hut. The whole gang moved. Boy, what a change. This new one has bricked-in ends instead of boarded-in ends. That's all, brother!

Wonder if you happened to read the article in the last Post . . . about Mustangs, and concerning the doings of this Col. Howard who put up such a good scrap a while ago. Took on some forty Jerry fighters single-handedly. Got himself a half-dozen and got home in one piece.

Probably be a lurid article in the *Chi. Herald American*. Neighbored with a correspondent the other night. Didn't tell this character anything, so maybe he won't write anything.

Maybe you noticed the story about Mustangs penetrating as far as Poland? Long haul, isn't it? Also says where a couple of '51s set up a speed record in the States, going from coast to coast in six and a half hours, 375 average for the trip. Not bad, but we've done better and faster.

Right now the sun is trying to shine, and there's a lovely fat rainbow arching up across the flying field. Mebbe I'll grab me a Jeep and take a run out to the bottom of that there rainbow, scout around and see if those pots of gold are anywhere handy. Kind of doubt it. Speaking of rainbows, there one thing I always like to see: when you're racing along over the top of a cloud deck, and the sun is above you, there appears on the top of the clouds a little shadow of your ship, around which appears a circular rainbow. They call it the "Pilot's Halo"—which is the only one he'll ever get, and a pretty thing to see.

May 19, '44

Well, howdy! After a five-day layoff, got back on the ol' job today. Flew a very interesting mission to Berlin in which we got 11 aerial victories and lost one. An amusing incident with Frank Greene on his last hop before a 30-day rest-and-return leave in the States. We'd been predicting dire things for him on this flight. Zonk! What happens? Dire things. A '109 makes a lightning-fast attack and first thing I notice is ol' Frank in a vertical po-

Robert Frascotti joined the 486th several months after it began combat operations
and was killed when his aircraft struck a control tower during a pre-dawn takeoff
on D-Day—June 6, 1944. Here's how Ted describes the event in his book *Bailout
over Normandy:* "All of a damned sudden a horrible, billowing explosion half-blinded
me, and I knew automatically what it was: a Mustang, a maximum load of high-
octane, and one of the boys all gone to glory in a puff of flame. I didn't know
who'd bought it, but I did know that it was a pilot of my squadron. Mac and I
circled the runway at 500 feet, just beneath the weeping overcast, and we watched
the flaring mess die away to glowing redness. With their pilots taking full advantage
of the grisly beacon, Mustangs shot from the blackness of the takeoff position to
gleam momentarily in the crash flames and disappear again as they became safely
airborne. [Later] we learned that it had been friend Scotti who hadn't made it off
the ground on takeoff . . . [We'd listened as he] cracked his last joke when he
climbed into his ship for takeoff. Looked into the black rainy night and hollered
'I'm surrounded by Assassins!' and gave with his battle cry of 'Umbriago!' On the
instrument takeoff he got a little off-course and barreled into a brick control tower
at 175 mph, disappearing in a puff of flame. Scotti and his Mustang and 450
gallons of 100-octane, all gone at once."

sition, twisting round and round in tight, fast corkscrew rolls. He'd been leading our flight and I brought up the rear. We'd been plenty high and my heater was busted, thusly frosting up my canopy and I'd been melting holes with my thumb, so as to see ahead. So Jerry passes me up in favor of getting the leader. So when Frank spins down I figger I'd best go look after him, so I split-ess down and tags along behind him at a fair rate of speed. He pulls out of the melee heading for home and I slide in alongside him, speaking reassuring words; and there he is, staggering for England with one flap shot away and a wheel hanging down. He is sweating considerably at this stage of the game, so I kid him along on the RT and we come on out together. I run out of oxygen pretty soon and turn Frank over to Colby who happens along, and he escorts him the rest of the way out. So I let down to thick air and have a little fun stooging around for the rest of the way back. Picked up a couple of Liberators over the North Sea and had a chat with them over the radio. Smoked a half pack of cigarettes and et a chocolate bar en route, as usual. Generally miss out lunch on these long missions, so get pretty hungry and a candy bar comes in handy.

Anyway, rather than bail out over home, Frank makes a wild 200 mph landing at a field near to our own, and tonight he's full of tall tales! He'll be home in the States pretty soon and I'll ask him to give you a call on the phone when he finds time. He lives in Providence. He's just plain lucky that this Hun didn't have a finer bead on him! Happened to note that it was fifty below zero at 25,000 feet today . . . about normal for that altitude. Have a darned good ship now, except for a few bugs in her yet.

Expect to pay another social call on Len tomorrow or next day. Nice having an old friend so close by. Didn't happen to escort his outfit today, but we saved the gang we did escort a lot of trouble. Inasmuch as I'm pooped tonight, think I'll retire and dream pleasant dreams . . . full of '109s with me on their tails . . .

May 24, '44
Recently have come to the conclusion that being a locomotive engineer in Nazi-land comes under the classification of being the Most Hazardous Job in the World. Railroaders' morale in the old country has struck a new all-time low, I bet. They've had it. Whooooo-Whooooooo . . . Berlin Express coming round the bend, goin' ninety miles an hour, and out of a clear blue sky comes a string of Mustangs . . . tat-a-tat-tat, and that's all, brother!

Those old armor-piercing .50s sure let the steam out of a boiler. Ho ho ho! Hit 'em in the right place and they don't just let steam out of holes, tho. Whole cockeyed locomotive goes blooey, which is quite something to view thru a gunsight. And troops, passengers, generals, the whole trainload of 'em sit right where they are for a while right out in the middle of no-place. Which thought tickles me somewhat. Heh.

In the delightful process of altering the RR situation over there, we've had some durned good hunting. Rather an easy game to track! Just drive down the main line 'til you find one. Then put a good squirt into the right spot and another valuable hunk of Jerry equipment is ready for the scrap pile. Now and then locate a nice juicy freight train, maybe chugging thru a small town, and might notice a flock of Huns scurrying around the streets . . . then we really put on an exhibition for 'em, ruining their engine and then working over the cars until the works is just one big, smoking, perforated mess. Then wave at the people and blow the joint. That must be a wee bit rough on their morale, seeing our leisurely forays right into their own backyard. I suppose they curse the Luftwaffe for not putting a stop to our bold work.

This train-busting is just a minor sideline anyway, looked upon by us as a relief from other more monotonous or more hazardous work. It's a lot of damn fun, but don't think our eyes aren't kept in the back of our heads all the time. The Luftwaffe is very much more dead in the news-papers than it is in actuality. They still have a powerful force of fighters, which they however try to conserve for attacking our long-range bombers. They're still a pretty sly bunch of citizens, so we take that into due consid-eration and never, never get at all sloppy in our flying over there. One gets careless only once in this racket. However reckless one of our deep fighter penetrations may seem, it's really a well-planned offensive flown by pilots who know the score and know the full value of aggressive teamwork.

Frank left for his 30 days in the States, along with a few other lads. I didn't make this trip, but may join the next few pilots to leave, which is a matter of three or four months, so don't get your blood pressure up.

Sure got a kick out of a little deal the other day. Happened to be down to about a hundred feet over a small town in central Germany with a cou-ple of empty gas tanks hanging under my wings. See a lot of the local pop-ulation running up and down Main Street, so aimed my ship at the city hall and dumped my tanks. Kicked my tail around so I could watch 'em fall and one of 'em went sailing thru some trees and bounced off the side of a frame house and the other lit plunk in the middle of the market square and raised a helluva cloud of dust. Heh heh. Probably scared hell out of the natives!

Have had the usual bouts with flak. Out of the twelve million, two hundred and fifty thousand rounds of heavy flak, light flak, twenty-mm, and assorted small-arms fire that has been aimed at me personally, each and every round has been either too low or too high, a bit behind or a bit in front of me. Ha. (Wot am *I* laughin' at?) Each black puff that explodes in my vicinity represents another couple of hundred bucks for the Nazi taxpayer's hard-earned moolah gone to pot. Any trigger-happy Jerry gunner who can come within fifty feet of my ship deserves another Iron Cross. (I'd like to make it a Marble Cross, meself.) For when I see them dirty black puffs begin to track me, I put on a show that'd take the trophy at the Cleveland Air Races. I have developed the most intricate and otherwise fancy brand of evasive action ever seen over Europe. Sometimes when I fly across the sky and over a city, I can look down and see a battery of four or eight muzzle flashes, and then I can make a small turn off course, and in a few seconds or so there'll be a fine barrage right where I would have been, had I not turned. When the situation is that simple, I gotta chuckle at 'em. Whee.

Am going on seven-day's leave with McKibben day after tomorrow. Will probably spend another day with Tommy and see how he's behavin'—as if I didn't know. Will see Len tonight or tomorrow. Tommy's in the 9th Air Force flying Thunderbolts, and he likes 'em as well as I did. But the poor guy ain't been exposed to Mustangs . . .

June 4, '44

Howdy! I've been sadly neglecting me duty of writing home . . . not a duty, but a joy! However, McKibben and I have been prowling about England on a seven-day leave, which is not conducive to letter writing, as you might well imagine.

Delighted to get the snapshots with your last letter. You look like a million bucks (or pounds, like they say over here. Heh.) Speaking of snapshots, here's one for you of me, taken by one of my crew. Caught me in an off moment while I wuz strollin' towards me ship, hands in pockets and a dull look on me pan . . .

Regarding the picture of Willie O. Jackson I sent home: you said he looked like a "fine-looking man." Well, today I was riding in the back seat of his jeep, en route to the mess hall, and I hollers, "Hey, Willie . . . my maw sez that you are a fine-looking man on account of I sent her your picture!" Well, he does a double-take and looks around at me with a simple grin and we all holler "Lookout, Willie!" because he is about to run down a GI who is walking down the road. We miss him by inches.

Saw Len while on my leave . . . spent the first afternoon and evening over at his base. Had another good session with him, and he hasn't a cock-eyed thing in the world to moan about, outside the fact that he drives a bomber instead of flying a fighter! He's well fed, available to a drink or two, well housed, and amongst good companions. On the two-meal-a-day situation, he is lucky. We generally sleep thru breakfast and have a candy bar for lunch. This candy bar is generally munched bit by bit. The process is as follows: I am at thirty-thousand feet, more or less, and hungry. I feel and fumble around in various pockets for a frozen bar of chocolate. I am scanning the skies meanwhile, looking for trouble and keeping formation at the same time, and simultaneously watching engine instruments, jockeying throttle, etcetera. I grab the candy bar finally, finding it mixed up with various odds and ends . . . cigarettes, matches, morphine kit, burn kit, money kit, escape kit, maps, etc. I then put the control stick between my knees, trim the ship to stand for this treatment, then stuff one corner of chocolate bar under the side of my oxygen mask. Takes some time to find my big mouth, and then I nibble off a hunk and remove the candy bar before I pass out for lack of oxygen. At this pernt, I am seeing black spots floating around in front of my eyes on account of because I have probably missed couple of sniffs of oxygen. This process I repeat as long as I please. Generally it isn't very long, for something always happens . . . either we spot some Nazzies and start operating, or we go into a wild series of acrobatics to dodge bombers or flak, whereupon I drop remnants of chocolate bar all over the cockpit into highly inaccessible places. Anyway, that is how I often eat lunch. (Quite different from strolling into Walgreens and ordering up a cheese sandwich, no doubt.) Get back home in time for supper, which might well be a slab of spam and some berled potaters and a cuppa java.

As for cigarettes, we get a pack a day rationed, but there are always non-smokers around who will give you their rations, which makes for a neat two packs a day, which I kin handle very well. I allus tear my oxygen mask off at the first possible moment when on a mission: for instance, if we go to Big B and then let down to the deck and go strafing, I take my mask off when we get down and light up a Lucky. Can't light a match much above fifteen thousand feet, by the way. No air. Strafing, I sit there and smoke and shoot and then light up another, and as soon as I get out over the North Sea again, headin' for home and sweating out my gas, I buzz the water and smoke up a half pack or so and have a wonderful time watching the world go by under my wings. Wot a life!

Dunno if Frank Greene will phone up, but he will send some flowers an account of I give him one pound ten shillings to do so. He's a good guy and one of the original Fightin' 21st Squadron pilots.

Spent the seven-day leave with Mac, just beating around the local countryside. We spent two nights in a fair-sized town nearby, which proved to be the friendliest town we've hit so far. Lodged in Ye Olde Red Lion Inne and slept in feather beds two feet thick. One morning in this town we are drinking ale in a quaint little pub and we get to jabbering with two native men. They invite us out to their home for the afternoon, so we take them up and pay this one gent a call. He and his wife showed us a fine, relaxing afternoon. We talked over America and England and relative customs and so on, hashed over the war and had a bit of scotch. His wife was very thoughtful and at tea time she served Mac and me one-each poached egg on toast with coffee. A real gesture, that, for the poor citizens get about one egg every six months to call their own. Fine people. Met all the neighbors and their kids and retired gracefully before supper time. Folks over here are so very strictly rationed that unexpected guests exert a great strain on the family larder.

This young couple had honeymooned on the Continent and had many travel folders, menus, and brochures to remember their travels by. It was evidently the high point of their lives and they glowed with happiness as they told us of their evenings in Paris and Berlin and so on. Mac and I enjoyed our visit with them immensely . . . our first actual insight into fairly normal British middle-class life.

In this same town we were met everywhere by friendliness, with none of the cold stares quite common to the larger cities that have been corrupted by the flood of Yanks. Matter of fact, we couldn't buy ourselves a drink in any of the pubs; some old gent would step up and take care of us, and try as we might we couldn't return the compliment. And there was one hilarious deal involved: Mac and I have a thirst one morning early. We scout all over town and finally find one pub open, down by the railroad tracks somewhere. We guzzle a jug of ale and swap lies with the local types, when all of a sudden a little one-pony cart hauls up outside and a little old man jumps out and hops into the joint. He is about seventy and has a reckless, wiry, frizzled moustache that sprouts in all directions. He carries a gold-knobbed walking stick and acts like a frisky old Civil War vet. Well, he drives in and sees Mac and me huddled in a corner. "Aha! Good fer ye, Yanks!" he cries. And he swishes his cane thru the air and shouts to his fellow Englishmen, "By Gad!" he sez, "these young Yankee airmen are better than our own boys! Far better! By Gad, I like 'em better'n you dam Englishmen! Got a lotta git-up and go to 'em!" So Mac and me, we laugh and ask the ol' guy to join us, but he just hooks down a quick gin and pays our bar check and hops out into his cart and takes off. Mac and I, being unpopular in this pub by now, we take off too, heading uptown. We stop in the first pub we find open and have a beer. Then in walks this same old geezer, and when he sees us he does a double-take and then hollers: "By gad, just seen a couple of your flying chums down in another pub! Fine lads! Fine boys they were. Bought 'em an ale! Have one on me. I like you Yanks better'n these dam Englishmen!" So we don't let on to the old guy that we were the same fliers he'd seen ten minutes before, and we drink up.

Well, we just drifted from town to town, partying here and there, meeting characters and so on, and we finish our leave in Norwich within lurching distance of our field.

So you dreamed I buzzed the old homestead, hey? You'll know when I do. If I ever come thru our backyard at 500 plus, it'll suck the keys right out of the piano, and that's no lie! And there won't be one damn leaf left on your peetunias. Not a one, if the job is done as it should be done. And I, nacherly, am just the gent who kin do 'er.

Don't expect me in two months, as you seem to do. Make it four or five, willya?

No chance to see Tom since the first visit to Kent. Will get down there eventually.

My new ship is a dandy. Did a little aerodynamic reconstruction work on her today! She didn't trim up quite right, so me and my crew chief bent the wingtips with a monkey wrench and that ought to take care of it. North

American Aircraft engineers would lose their minds if they spent a week with us!

If you can find me a flask I'll be quite happy, as the one I carry only holds about one good slug. And if I'm floating around playing sailor in the Ditch, I sure as hell will be able to do with more than one nip!

Hope Russ comes out O.K. I probably know more about it, and knew before you, on account of in this Air Force there is one big grapevine working, and business news travels fast. Every day we all hear stories of our pals in China and India and Italy and so on . . . News comes by word of mouth, letters, etc. Casual conversations with ferry pilots often bring out news of pilots we all know. Verra inresting.

Mac and I pulled a Wise One the other day. We'd been on a milk-run bomber escort mission and on the way home we wuz bored stiff, so we spot a flight of four of our gang about ten thousand feet below us. We dive plenty fast and go down behind 'em and under 'em and pull up in front (about ten feet in front) and slow-roll straight up, scaring hell out of these birds and busting up their neat formation nicely. Corky (Corcoran) hollers at us, scared and sore as all hell, "You crazy blank-blankey blankety blanks!" And we push our mike buttons and give 'em a nasty laugh. Ho ho!

Enclosed find an odd English banknote that I want you cash in and spend on an evening downtown or somewheres . . . five pounds equals twenty bucks and that ought to wine and dine you to your heart's content. I won it in a crap game, so forget it. Won't have you putting it away, so be sure and have it all gone real quick, willya?

So long and mucho love to one and all . . .

Chapter 15

· ·

The End of the Joker

June 22, '44

WESTERN UNION
Washington D.C. 9:13 a.m. June 22
To: Francis M. Fahrenwald
10330 S. Hamilton

THE SECRETARY OF WAR DESIRES ME TO EXPRESS
HIS DEEP REGRET THAT YOUR BROTHER FIRST
LIEUTENANT THEODORE FAHRENWALD HAS BEEN
REPORTED MISSING IN ACTION SINCE 8 JUNE OVER
FRANCE. IF FURTHER DETAILS OR OTHER INFORMA-
TION ARE RECEIVED YOU WILL BE PROMPTLY NOTI-
FIED.
ULIO—ADJUTANT GENERAL

Aug. 14, '44

WESTERN UNION
Intl-CD Sansorigine Via WUCABLES 14 Aug 925P 11:53 a.m.
Mrs. Marjorie Fahrenwald 11538 Longwood Drive Chgo.
WELL AND HAPPY LOVE
TED FAHRENWALD

Aug. 24, '44

Hello . . . Long time no write, but I ain't been exactly what you'd call available! Hope you received the cablegram I sent, for I rather think that the Army telegram will take some time getting there.

I'm now back amongst the ol' gang . . . Mac and Rocky and Joe . . . and it's sure good to be with them again. Chances are I'll be walking down Longwood Drive before long, looking for 11538. As usual, don't count too much on it, but I don't think it'll be long now.

Am fat and sassy again . . . been eating like mad and smoking cigarettes making up for lost time. Had quite a reunion with the boys last night in the Club. A scotch-and-soda or two!!!

Am thru with combat flying for the time being, so you don't have to ponder that situation for a spell. Just playing around with these flying machines around the field. We have a couple of light ships and I've been taking some of the ground crew up for stunt rides, running around picking up stranded pilots, etc.

Am all out of practice at this letter-writing stuff, so this'll be a short one tonight. Will try to write again soon, but there really isn't much to write about, as I'm leading a very dull life at present.

Leo Northrop and Corcoran and a few others have gone home for a while. Frank Greene got back yesterday and told me he'd called you. Glad he did, for no doubt he told you to relax and wait for me to write you again.

About bedtime, and I can't keep all these hard-working pilots awake with the noise that Mac's typewriter makes. I'll be lurching thru the front door one of these days. So long . . .

To find out in suspenseful and hilarious
detail about Ted's exploits between
June 8—when he parachuted out of
his burning Mustang over Normandy
into the waiting arms of the French
Resistance—and August 14, when
he cabled his family back home
about his survival, read
*Bailout Over Normandy: A Flyboy's
Adventures with the French Resistance
and Other Escapades in Occupied France*
by Ted Fahrenwald

Published by Casemate Publishers

288 PAGES • 978-1-61200-157-9 •
$29.95 • HARDCOVER

Also available in eBook format